To **Hell**
With Hell

It's About Time

Ellwood W. Norquist

Cosmic Connection Publishing   Tucson, Arizona

Cosmic Connection Publishing
1540 S. Aida Avenue
Tucson, AZ 85710

This edition was prepared for printing by
Ghost River Images
5350 East Fourth Street
Tucson, Arizona 85711
www.ghostriverimages.com

Cover design by Ellwood W. Norquist

ISBN 978-0-9646995-4-0

Library of Congress Control Number: 2016944250

Printed in the United States of America
First Printing: July, 2016

Acknowledgements

First, I would like to thank Jamie Garrick, John Dommisse and Hollis Toal who read my drafts with editor's eyes helping my final words to be more descriptive and flow more smoothly.

Much appreciation and many thanks to my friend, Bruce Gregory, for the two informative and inspiring essays found in the Appendix. Bruce is well known for his work with Charles Lehman, author of the recently published book, *The Book Of Andrew*.

I would like to express my thanks to Amazon for making me aware of and to supply me with the many books I needed to help me in my research.

Also, thanks to those at Simutek (Apple) who kept my computer running in good shape to complete my manuscript.

And, yes, thanks to Michael White of Ghost River Images for his patience with my many changes in the manuscript and in working with designing the cover.

Dedication

To all Souls who
fear the pains of a Hell
for themselves or for a loved one

Contents

Also by Ellwood W. Norquist

We Are One: A Challenge to Traditional Christianity (1995)

All That Is and All That Isn't: Reconciling Quantum Physics, Philosophy and Spirituality (2010)

Who Are We? Science And Spirit Answering With One Voice (2014)

Introduction

The title of Ellwood Norquist's book, *To Hell With Hell*, expresses the freeing impact on one's mind of the biblical truth that Hell is neither a literal fire nor a geographical location. Biblically speaking, Hell is an explanation of the truth that all people, at the end of life, are accountable for how they have treated others in this life. Christianity calls this accountability "reaping what you sow." In the Eastern Religions such accountability is called "Karma." What Norquist has written is in accord with what Pope Francis stated in 2013, in the papal office three months: #1. There is no literal burning hell. #2. Jesus died for all people, so everyone is redeemed.

For readers who understand allegories, anthropomorphic language, metaphors, hyperbole, and other such literary devices, The Holy Bible, with crystal clarity, teaches Christian Universalism. Since religious (vs. spiritual) people tend to be literalists and legalists, they often miss the spiritual truth expressed in beautiful, bountiful cross-cultural, timeless symbolic language. When fire is logically understood as symbolizing purification, all major religions, and various minor ones, teach universal salvation. The best example of this truth is Jesus' mixed metaphor stating the purpose of this karmic experience called "hell": "For every one shall be salted with fire" (KJV) of which the best translation is in *The Good News Bible* (Also published as: *Good News Translation, Today's English Version*), "Everyone will be purified by fire." This sane and sensible explanation is verified by near-death and out-of-body death experiences (reported from across the USA and around the world), the validity of which I have explained, giving real-life examples, in both of my books.

In *To Hell With Hell*, Norquist goes into the scientific basis of understanding God's love is all-inclusive, unconditional, and ever-lasting. He addresses such mind-opening, and even mind-boggling scientific concepts as: the universe as a holograph, parallel universes (perhaps an infinite number of them), time (per Einstein) the past, present, and future happening simultaneously, quantum physics, the mind creating reality, reincarnation, global consciousness, etc. Since I am not a scientist, I cannot vouch for the validity of this scientific information. I do encourage readers to read with an open, inquiring mind, per the admonition of the great English philosopher, Sir Francis Bacon, (1561-1626), "Read not to contradict and confute, nor to believe and take for granted . . . but to weigh and consider."

As a seminary graduate, an Ordained Christian Minister, and Board Certified Chaplain, I can verify that the Greek New Testament teaches the truth of Christian Universalism. As a Board Certified Counselor, in a psychiatric hospital, and a hospice chaplain, providing spiritual care at the end of life to terminally ill patients, I have given many examples of fear-based religion as spiritual abuse/terrorism/insanity.

Boyd C. Purcell, Ph.D., author
Spiritual Terrorism: Spiritual Abuse from the Womb to the Tomb and *Christianity Without Insanity: For Optimal Mental/Emotional/Physical Health*

Ellwood Norquist has just shared with me the pre-print proof of his new book, *To Hell With Hell*. As with his previous book, *Who Are We?* Norquist shows evidence of an inquiring mind and a journey into answers. His annotated chapters lead the reader into a logical treatise concerning what he and I believe to be marketing tools of the church, and should the reader have an open mind he or she will be left with the utter impossibility of a God of love creating anything that would cause fear or torment.

His writing confirms a very well-read and educated mind that unfolds his subject in very logical manner. Should everyone read this book? Certainly not someone who is steeped in a belief system that is founded on a capricious and vindictive God . . . unless he or she starts to think and reason that most of what was believed has been presented by they who know not and know not that they know not. Yes, *To Hell With Hell* will be enjoyed by people who relish being challenged and who are thinkers in their own right.

I give it a double thumbs up!

Larry A. Swartz
Co-minister, Unity of Tucson

Preface

I was born to question.

I came into this world with Christian parents in a rural community in Minnesota.

Our small church was a member of the Swedish Baptist Conference of America. As Baptists we were taught to love God, but in more stringent and threatening tones we were told to fear Him. And, oh! how the weekly sermons (twice on Sunday, and often a mid-week service) of "hell, fire and brimstone" helped to instill fear! Then, too, there were those frightening pictures of hell in that book in my uncle's house – Dante's *Divine Comedy: Heaven, Hell, and Purgatory*.

Could I love that God? The one who created me but had also created a hell to which He would send me, to be tortured for ever and ever - and ever - if I did not live up to his demands.

Too, on my bedroom wall (a room shared with my two-year older brother) my mother had placed a plaque reading "The Fear of the Lord is the Beginning of Wisdom." [1] I did not need that daily reminder: The sermons at church were accomplishing that quite well!

My young mind just could not reconcile the contradiction. I could not love someone I feared.

In my early years there were some strange things that happened

---

1   I learned later that that quotation from Proverbs 9:10, in new translations of
     the scriptures reads "to stand in awe of God is the beginning of wisdom."

which I could not understand or explain, which now I would call psychic or paranormal. From time to time my mother had confided in me, telling me about strange happenings in her life, so in a sense, I was prepared for accepting unexplainable experiences. I suspect that my mother recognized in me a soul that would understand.

One event that concerned me at the time was at the age of five or six, or at least old enough to know that I had better not tell anyone about it: One hot summer night I was lying on the grass in our yard looking up at the star-filled heavens. My vision became fixated on a group of seven stars. I began to sob, the tears flowing, and I murmuring, "I want to go home, I want to go home." "Home" was that group of seven stars. Suddenly I recovered and realized that I was at home, home with my family. "What was I thinking"?

Some days after, I asked someone if that group of seven stars had a name. I was told that the group was called the "Seven Sisters". Later I learned that it was the constellation of the Pleiades. That whole event was forgotten for many years until one day when I spied on a bookstore table, "The Pleiadian Agenda" by Barbara Hand Glow. I bought it. I read it. I got answers!

For twelve months while in the Army Air Force I was in a special study program of mathematics and physics at Washington University in St. Louis. This began an interest in physics, but my more compelling interests were and still are in history, international affairs, politics and spirituality. Later, my bachelor's degree at the University of Minnesota was in International Relations.

Later, after twelve years as a purser with Trans World Airlines, traveling to European capitals two to three times monthly, I returned to school for a master's degree in History at Columbia University in New York City and then, for twelve years, taught Ancient and Renaissance History at Horace Mann School in New York City.

During my years in the military and for many years after, I had stopped reading the Bible. One day I decided to once again read it, especially the New Testament, reading it with an open mind, reading it for what it really said, not for what I had been, as a youth, brainwashed to believe.

I read, read and re-read. Those "truths" that I had been indoctrinated with in my early years, I just did not find! I went to the local Baptist Church in my neighborhood in Brooklyn and sought out the pastor and told him the problem. His shocking reply: "You cannot find those concepts in the Bible because they are not in the Bible."

Holy Cow!

Thoroughly shocked, I blurted out, "Why don't you tell your congregation the truth?" Not exactly appreciating the question, but answering honestly, he said, "If I tell them the truth on a Sunday morning, I will be fired before Monday morning."

Wow, wow and wow!

After many happy and wonderful years, first in Manhattan and then in Brooklyn, I retired and moved to Tucson, Arizona. With more leisure time, the bookstores were calling me loudly. I answered. I began reading, pen in hand, underlining and commenting in the margins. Most of the books were on science and spirituality and I re-doubled my study of "A Course In Miracles," [2] which I had acquired in New York City the moment it was published in 1976 .

All this reading led to a couple of years teaching a non-credit course reconciling science and spirituality at Pima Community College in Tucson The good response I received from my students, mostly middle aged adults, encouraged me to write my first book, *We Are One: A Challenge to Traditional Christianity* (1995), later in 2010 to write *All That is and All That Isn't: Reconciling Quantum Physics, Philosophy and Spirituality*, and in 2014, *Who are We? Science and Spirit Answering with One Voice*.

Then, after celebrating my 92nd birthday, with not even a thought of ever again putting pen to paper, I awoke one morning with an inner voice saying that I must keep on writing. I shouted out loud, "What the hell would I write about?" Instantly I heard a response, "hell". Again out loud I yelled, "to hell with hell". The inner voice answered calmly and clearly, "That is the title of your book." So, here it is: *To Hell With Hell. It's About Time*.

If having this book in print will help just one person to lose his

---

2 Please see Appendix Number One for information about "A Course In Miracles"

tormenting fears of everlasting punishment it will be well worth it.

On, then, to Chapter 1 where we will briefly look at some of the topics to be developed more thoroughly in later chapters.

Part I

To Hell With Hell

"Unthinking respect for authority is the greatest enemy of truth"
–Albert Einstein

"Sit down before fact like a little child and be prepared to give up preconceived notions, follow humbly wherever and whatever abyss nature leads, or you will learn nothing."
–T. A. Huxley

"Faith is believing something you know ain't so."
–Mark Twain."

Chapter 1: Introducing the Subject

I begin with these words. "There is no Hell." I will end with these words, "There is no Hell"

Throughout man's life on this planet, it seems that he has believed in some kind of punishment for his sins. Especially in the western world, we have been taught, and so many have accepted, the idea of an everlasting punishment in a "hell". And how terribly we have suffered because of it. One Christian pastor who grappled for years with his church's teaching about hell puts it this way: "Living in such anxiety about one's eternal destiny is itself spiritually abusive and even terroristic." [1] And a Russian theologian has this to say: "I can conceive of no more powerful and irrefutable arguments in favor of atheism than the eternal torments of hell." [2] Is it not about time that we say, "to hell with hell".

There is a very important question that needs an answer before we direct our attention to our subject of hell. You will understand this question better when reading part II, but let's take a quick first look at it. The question is "Who are you"? In answering, first consider these preliminary questions: Do you have a body? Do you have a mind? Do you have a soul? If you answer "yes" to all three, then I ask, who are you that has those three things? You are not what you have. The answer, of course is that you do not have a soul. You ARE a soul!! You are a soul temporarily housed in your body.

Another factor to consider is the question of reincarnation. Jesus believed in reincarnation During the historical period of the life of Jesus in Palestine, reincarnation was an accepted doctrine, especially among the Essenes. Jesus reminded his disciples that the Scriptures foretold the return of Elijah and that he was there with them in the body of John the Baptist. A thought to keep in mind: If one is a great sinner in one life, then a veritable saint in another, what then? Throughout our earthly lives we are always the same soul.

Another thing to consider, perhaps the most compelling, certainly the most easily understood, is that God is a God of love and He created us in HIS IMAGE, his Sons and Daughters. Can it be even considered that our heavenly Father would consign us to an eternal punishment? We may be prodigal sons and daughters now but when we finally remember who we are, we will return home. In this Introduction we have spoken briefly about things that will be dealt with in more detail as we proceed and in Part II, especially, we will come to a full understanding of who we are and realize that a hell or any kind of punishment by our creator is not even conceivable.

1. Purcell, Boyd C., *Spiritual Terrorism*, p.15
2. Nicholas Berdayaev, quoted in Steve Gregg, *All You Want To Know About Hell*, p. 1.

Chapter 2: Our Casual Use of the Word "Hell"

If hell is a frightening thought to millions of people on earth, we do not seem to be aware of that in our daily lives. Let us, in a light mood, look at some of the casual ways we use the word,"hell" in our conversations.

In jest or in argument:
    The hell, you say
    Oh, go to hell

In anger
    Go to hell
    To hell with you
    May you burn in hell

In agreement
    Hell, yes
    Hell, no

In questioning or in astonishment
    What the hell! Are you crazy? or, What do you mean by that?

In England at the time of the writing of the King James version of the Bible, the word "hell" was used both as a noun and as a verb. A farmer might have said, "Tomorrow we are going to put our potatoes in hell" or " Tomorrow we are going to hell our potatoes." Of course, using the word simply meant a hole in the ground. Keep this in mind when you are reading the Bible.

"Fear of eternal punishment is demonic and spiritually terroristic."
–Boyd C. Purcell

"Be ye therefore merciful as your Father is merciful."
–St Luke 6:33.

"God is spirit and those who worship him must worship in spirit and truth."

Chapter 3: Christianity's Views of Hell

Roman Catholicism, Eastern Orthodox, as well as the numerous versions of Protestantism, all entertain some version of a punishment in a hell.

Catholics in general have a purgatory as well as a hell of infinite misery. The idea of a purgatory was learned largely from the Etruscans and from Dante's Divine Comedy. [1]

Protestant Christians have a hell of punishment for everyone who does not accept Jesus as their personal savior. So, let us take a brief look at the basic Christian views of hell.

I. TRADITIONAL VIEW

This view teaches that there is eternal punishment of a burning hell, the most gruesome torment imaginable. This concept was taught by St. Augustine, Thomas Aquinas and other early church leaders. It is still taught today by the evangelicals and fundamentalists.

It is a concept and teaching that terrorizes many today, especially the youth growing up in a family with a church environment where each Sunday they are threatened from the pulpit with a hell of eternal punishment. This is now said to be one of the causes of teen age suicide. Some may, on the other hand, respond as did Charles Darwin. In his autobiography he made this comment.

> "I can hardly see how anyone ought to wish Christianity to be true; for if so the plain language of the text seems to show that the men who do not believe, and this would include my Father, Brother and almost all of my friends, will be everlastingly punished. And this is a damnable doctrine." [2]

A famous pastor and professor in a fundamentalist Seminary who grappled for years in overcoming his belief in hell has this to say.

> "If the doctrine of eternal punishment is true, God is not just, holy, or righteous. The abusers, who are literalists and legalists, have it backwards. The fact that God is holy, just, and righteous is exactly why God will not torture people at all, much less forever." [3]

II. ANNIHILATION

Seventh Day Adventists adhere to the view of annihilation. They believe that after a period of punishment the dead will eventually pass from existence.

Jehovah's Witnesses believe that 144,000 souls will go to heaven. Some few of Jehovah's Witnesses will remain on earth forever in an earthly paradise. The rest of humanity will just die and be no more.

I find these views little better than the fundamentalist view. What God has created is forever. He created us, his Sons and Daughters, in His own likeness. We are without blemish. Yes, we may be prodigal Sons and Daughters now, but when we finally remember who we are we will return to the arms of our Creator. It matters nothing which religion you belong to nor what you believe or whether you are an atheist in your present life. Eventually everyone, as Sons and Daughters of God, will return to heaven, which in true reality, we never left. All of our lives on earth are just part of our dream of separation. This will be explained further in Part II.

III. RECONCILIATION

Two early scholars of Christendom, Clement of Alexandria (150-215) and Origen (185-251), were adherents of reconciliation, the idea that all will be saved.

Clement of Alexandria, born in Athens to pagan parents and a student of Plato, believed and taught that everybody would be saved eventually. He was declared a saint by the Eastern Catholic Church and by the Anglican Church. He was also considered a saint by the Roman Church until he was removed from sainthood by Pope Sixtus V.

Origen, being a student of Clement of Alexandria, also taught the idea of a final reconciliation of all souls. He was never canonized by the Church because of that belief.

One of today's proponents of reconciliation has this to say:

> "Unending torment speaks to me as sadism,
> not justice ... It is a doctrine that makes the
> Inquisition look reasonable. It all seems a
> flight from reality and common sense," [4]

The concept of reconciliation is an improvement over the view of an everlasting torment in hell, but it still gives the idea of a God who believes in some form of a punishment for what is called sin. A renowned Christian leader has this to say:

> "No evangelical, I think, need hesitate to
> admit that in his heart of hearts he would like

universalism to be true. Who can take plea-
sure in the thought of people being eternally
lost? If you want to see folks damned, there
is something wrong with you."[5]

To close this chapter, I would like to quote a very famous Eng-
lishman, C. S. Lewis, who wrote these words:

"There is no doctrine I would more willingly
remove from Christianity than hell, if it lay
in my power.. . I would pay any price to be
able to say truthfully: 'All will be saved.'"[6]

In the next chapter we will discuss what the Bible has to say
about hell.

1. This will be discussed in Chapter 5
2. Charles Darwin, *The Autobiography of Charles Darwin* 1809-
   1882. London: Collins, 1958, p. 201.
3. Boyd C. Purcell, Spiritual Terrorism, *Author House. 1663 Liberty
   Drive, Bloomin*gton, Indiana, 4703, 2008, p. 201.
4. John Wenham, *Facing Hell: A Story Of A Nobody.* Carlisle Cum-
   bria; Paternoster, Press, p. 251.
5. Kenneth Kantzer and Carl F. H. Henry: *Evangelical Affirmations*
   (Grand Rapids: Zondervan,1990, pp. 107-108.
6. C.S, Lewis, *The Problem of Pain* (London: Geoffrey Bles, 1940),
   94.

"For he is kind unto the unthankful and to the evil."
–St. John 6:35

"All die in Adam all live in Christ and God, the Father shall become all in all."
–1 Corinthians 15:21-28

Chapter 4: Hell in the Bible

A traditional hell as generally taught by both Roman Catholicism and Protestantism is not found in the Bible. Oh yes, the word, "hell" appears very often in both the Old Testament and the New Testament, especially in the King James version of the scriptures.

But, did you ever question why the word, hell, was used to translate so many different words meaning so many different concepts?

I would like to begin this discussion by quoting the words of a protestant Christian pastor and biblical scholar who spent years in agony over the question of hell.

> "The word 'hell' is nowhere to be found in the extant manuscripts of the Hebrew Old Testament, or in the Septuagint, i.e., Greek Old Testament, or in the Greek New Testament. And further, none of following named biblical heroes ever said a word about a so-called 'hell': Noah, Abraham, Moses, David, Jeremiah, John, Peter, Paul and most especially, Jesus. That's right! I did say that Jesus never spoke the word 'hell' in any language. [1]

In our English texts, the word "hell" is used to translate three different words meaning three different things in the original texts: "sheol", "hades", and "gehenna". Not one of these three words in the original texts translates to any teaching of an after death punishment

When the King James version of the bible was published in 1611 A.D., the word hell simply indicated a hole in the ground. For example, a farmer might say "Tomorrow we are going to hell our potatoes" or "Tomorrow we are going to put our potatoes in hell." The word was used both as a verb and a noun. Personally, as a youth growing up on a farm, we raised our own garden potatoes and to keep them fresh for winter use, we would put them under the soil in a basement room that had no flooring. We put them "in hell".

The word, "sheol," in the original Hebrew of the Old Testament, meant the grave, while the word, "hades" was the Greek word for sheol or the grave. "Gehenna" was the word for the garbage dump outside of Jerusalem. We will look at these terms later.

HELL IN THE OLD TESTAMENT

Oh yes, the word "Hell" appears in the Old Testament many times. A contradiction? Not really, if you read the text to see what is actually being said and how it is translated into our English texts.

The Hebrew text uses the word, "Sheol", generally referring to the grave. The word is translated as the "grave" 35 times, as "hell" 31 times and as the "pit" 3 times. Let's look at examples in the Old Testament where the word, Sheol is translated into those words grave, hell and pit.

Psalms 49:14 "Like sheep they are laid in the 'grave' death shall feed upon them."

Psalms 9:17 "The wicked shall be turned into 'hell' and all the nations that forget God."

Psalms 69:15 "Let not the waterflood overflow me, neither let the deep swallow me up and not let the 'pit' shut her mouth upon me."

We are ready to move on to the New Testament where there is

much more to consider. Let us leave the Old Testament with this thought in Proverbs 10:12: "Hatred stirreth up strife, but love covereth all sins."

HELL IN THE NEW TESTAMENT

Have you been saved? Most fundamentalist Christians are asked that question and often too, ask that question of others. Growing up in a Baptist family and attending a church service twice on Sunday and a mid-week prayer meeting, I too, was often asked that question. And, yes, I asked that question of others. I answered an altar call and was "saved" and then baptized at age 14. During the next few years I began to realize that I had been saved before I was "saved" because in fact, I had never been lost. I began to realize that we, all of us, are children of God, and always have been and always will be.

> "God has saved us and called us with a holy calling, not according to our works, but according to his own purpose and grace which was given us in Christ Jesus before the world began." II Timothy 1:9

After reading that, I celebrate Jesus' last words on the cross, "It is finished."

Some interesting facts to keep in mind when reading the New Testament.

1. The Gospel of John has not one reference to a hell.

2. In the book of The Acts, the word hell appears twice, referring to the grave.

3. The word hell never comes up in apostolic preaching.

4. Whenever you read the word "hell" in the Bible keep in mind that the word simply meant a hole in the ground.

As I recall from my youth, there were members of our church and others who seemed to actually want there to be a hell of punishment for the people who frequented the dance halls and taverns, really for anyone who actually enjoyed living. They seldom smiled or seemed content in any way. So, to those readers who are skeptics and dare I say, "want" to believe in a hell of punishment, please consider this passage in I Peter 8 : 32-39.

> "If God is on our side, who is against us . "It is God who pronounces acquittal; Then what can separate us from the love of Christ ... that there is nothing in death or life, In the realm of spirit or superman powers, in the world as it is or the world as it shall be, in the forces of the universe, in heights or depths -nothing in all of creation that can separate us from the love of God in Christ Jesus our Lord."

And, let's add this scripture in Ephesians 4:4-6

> "There is one body and one Spirit, as also there is one hope held out in God's call to you; one Lord, one faith ,one baptism; one God and Father of all, Who is over all and through all and in all."

I hear some readers objecting, bringing up a long list of torments promised in the Second Epistle of Peter. But did you miss these words in the same letter?

> "... because it is not his will for any to be lost, but for all to come to repentance." (II Peter 3:9)

Can anyone or anything go contrary to God's will?

In any event, the book of II Peter was not an accepted book in the scriptures until at the council of Trent in 1625, it was added to the canon, the list of authorized books of the Bible. The Epistle is believed to have been written by an unknown author about 200 years after the first Epistle of Peter was written. The Epistle uses language that was not current in Peter's day. The book, today, is not accepted by most Christian scholars.

KARMA

We usually think of karma as being a belief of those in the East, but it is becoming more understood and accepted in the West.

In Galatians 6:7 we read: "Be not deceived, God is not mocked: for whatsoever a man soweth, that shall he also reap." In fundamentalist Christianity, a person who has lived a very sinful life can on his deathbed accept Jesus as his personal savior and be "saved". Where did he reap what he had sewn? Where or when did he suffer karma? If we consider reincarnation, he will suffer his karma in his succeeding lives on earth and finally, as it is for us all, he will return to his father, God.

GEHENNA

"The Israelis have cleaned up 'hell' and turned it into a parkland."(1)

Gehenna, in ancient Greek was the name of the garbage dump just outside the walls of Jerusalem. In Hebrew it was known as Gehinnom. The earliest biblical reference to Gehinnom is in II Chronicles 28:3--6.

Both in Matthew 5:29 and in Mark 9:43 the garbage dump Gehenna is translated as "hell" so it is this "hell" that modern Israel has turned into a green park.

In view of these and other mistranslations using the word "hell" when referring to the grave and even to a garbage dump should give one pause when reading the English translations of the scriptures.

Perhaps a word should be said about the biblical use of the words "unquenchable fire". In both the old and new testaments, those words are used to describe any large fire such as a forest fire.

PREDESTINATION

Later, in a separate chapter we will take an extended look at the subject of reincarnation but now let us consider the words in the Bible on the subject of predestination. If from the very beginning of time we were created by our father God, to be with him forever, where is the possibility of any punishment in a hell? Note these biblical references to predestination.

Ephesians I: 4-6
> "According as he hath chosen us in him before the foundation of the world, that we should be holy and without blame before him in love, having predestinated us unto the adoption of children by Jesus Christ to himself, according to the good pleasure of his will, to the praise of the glory of his grace."

And in verse 11 of the same chapter:
> "In whom also we have obtained an inheritance being predestinated according to the purpose of him who worketh all things after counsel of his own will.

Then in I Timothy 1 :9-10:
> "It is he who brought us salvation and called us to a dedicated life, not for any merit of ours, but of his own purpose and his own grace, which was granted to us in Christ Jesus from all eternity."

In the next chapter we will look at Dante's "Divine Comedy" which is one of the principal factors in the church's teaching of a hell.

1) "On one of my visits to Jerusalem, I stood atop its massive walls overlooking the city and environs. In the distance I noticed a particular park-like area where young couples were picnicking . . . Surprised by all the green grass in an otherwise semi-arid surrounding, I asked my guide about it. He replied, 'Oh, that's Gehenna, the place where the ancient city dump of Jerusalem was once situated; the traditional site of hell. . . Modern Israelis have cleaned up the property there for more enjoyable and environmentally-friendly purposes.' . . . Did he really say what I thought he had said–that the Israelis had cleaned up 'hell' and turned it into a parkland?"

–Ivan S. Rogers, *Dropping Hell And Embracing Grace*, Outskirts Press, Inc., Denver, Colorado, 2012.

Chapter 5: All Hope Abandon, Ye Who Enter In

Welcome to Hell. Dante will be your guide. He will show you through all the nine levels of hell. You will be safe with him as you witness the various levels of torture and eternal damnation.

BUT FIRST

Dante's writing is what gave you the hell that you learned in your Christian Church, the hell your minister threatens you with each time you listen to one of his fiery sermons. Dante's famous work, "The Divine Comedy: Heaven, Hell and Purgatory", was written in the early 14th century A.D. Dante died in 1321.

For over 700 years our western world has suffered because of the words of Dante's book of fiction. First, under Catholicism and continued under the Reformed Church begun by Martin Luther in 1519 when he posted his 95 Theses on the Wittenburg, Germany's church door. Luther and his fellow theologians, in their break from the established Church, declared there was no such place as Purgatory since they didn't find it in the Scriptures. Then they considered also doing away with Hell as they did not find any real evidence for it in the Scriptures. But wait! They relented, believing that if they did away with the punishment of hell, their benches in church would be empty and no longer, each Sunday, would they gather in the tithes and offerings.

Dante called his work "La Comedia" (The Comedy). The word "Divine" was added later by Boccaccio [1] and for all time since it has been known as "The Divine Comedy."

Dante's book is not divine and it is not a comedy. "The whole thing is like another scripture, and has functioned that way for centuries." [1]

It seems that the question readers might begin to ask is "Why did Dante's words describing a hell become so entrenched in our western world's imagination? One recent writer gives an answer. "Cleverly using Virgil and lots of junky myth, Dante is the one who made eternal punishment exotic and real, as well as Christian." [2]

The Roman Catholic Church fully embraced Dante's work for it certainly presented enough scary material to keep their followers coming each Sunday to their magnificent edifices and to fill their coffers with silver.

Dante grew up in the area of Italy inhabited by the Etruscans before the Romans took over. Their colorful religion entertained a belief in a Heaven, a Hell, and a Purgatory. These Etruscan beliefs helped to prepare Dante to incorporate those ideas with his knowledge of Greek and Roman mythology, especially Hesiod's "Theogony," Virgil's "Aeneid" and Ovid's Metamorphosis.

You are now at the entrance to the vestibule of Hell and you read those threatening words, "All Hope Abandon, Ye Who Enter In." You are with Dante who is guided by Vergil, one of the inhabitants of hell.

As you descend through the nine levels, you are not to suffer the horrible descriptions of the torments of the damned, but simply witness the sins of those in each descending level.

---

1 Boccaccio is best remembered for his bawdy book, The Decameron.

Level 1. Limbo Here are the good souls who lived and died before the death and resurrection of Jesus.

Level 2. The Lustful. You see Achilles here.

Level 3. The Gluttonous

Level 4. The Greedy

Level 5. The Angry Souls. They fight here for eternity in waters of fire.

Level 6. The Heretics

Level 7. The Violent - to others or to themselves. The Blasphemous

Level 8. The Fraudulent - The seducers and the astrologers. The astrologers are forced to run forward with their heads on backwards. The can only see where they have been but never where they are going.

Level 9. The Last and lowest cycle. Judas Iscariot is here. Satan is here, but separate from anybody, almost in a level of his own.

If any reader really wants to read the horrible details of each level, the book is available in any public library or you may prefer to ask your pastor to borrow his copy.

In our next chapter we will take a rather thorough look at the subject of reincarnation.

1. Jon M. Sweeney, *Inventing Hell: Dante, The Bible and Eternal Punishment*, Jericho Books, Hachette Book Group, 237 Park Ave, New York, N.V., p. 9.

2. Ibid., p. 3.

⚛

The Body of B. Franklin, Printer
Like the Cover of an old book
Its Contents torn out,
And stripped of its lettering and gilding
Lies here, food for worms;
Yet the work itself shall not be lost,
For it will (as he believed)
Appear once more
In a new and more beautiful edition
Corrected and amended
By the AUTHOR
                    —Benjamin Franklin

"I have been here before,
But when or how I cannot tell:
I know the grass before the door,
The sweet keen smell,
The sighing sound, the lights around the shore,
You have been mine before,
How long ago I may not know:
But just when at that swallow's soar
Your neck turned so,
Some vail did fall, – I knew it all of yore."
                    —Dante Gabriel Rossetti

Chapter 6: On Reincarnation

"I hold that when a person dies
His soul returns again to earth;
Arrayed in some new fresh disguise,
Another mother gives him birth,
With sturdier limbs and brighter brain
The old soul takes the road again."
–John Masefield

In the Old Testament Book of Job the question is asked, "If a man die, will he live again?"

What is your answer? Do you believe that you have lived before? Have you ever visited a city or a foreign land where things felt strangely familiar? Or perhaps on meeting someone for the first time you feel like you have known him or her forever? Well, maybe you have been in that city or foreign land before. Just maybe you have known that new friend a long time ago in a former life.

Reincarnation. The question as to whether the soul returns to this physical world in a new body after spending time in the between life is one that has been debated for many centuries. The Eastern peoples accept reincarnation as logical truth, understanding that they return again and again to a physical body until all karma is worked out. We in the West are more ambivalent about it, but polls taken over the past years show that a majority of us are beginning to accept the concept.

David Wilcock, who is believed by many to be the reincarnation of Edgar Cayce, writes that "There is abundant scientific evidence that we survive physical death and have already experienced multiple lifetimes on earth." [1]

Edgar Cayce, who was known as the "sleeping prophet", died in 1945. Over 500 books were written about him and the messages which he gave while asleep. More than 2,500 of his readings involved past lives. While in trance sleep he spoke fluently in twenty-four different languages, the languages of his questioners.

Cayce's readings gave a lot of evidence that we often reincarnate in familiar groups, returning over and over again in the same family and in the same circle of friends, but with different relationships, to work out problems that were left unresolved in our former relationships. For example, as Gina Cerminara wrote in *Many Mansions*, "No marriage is a start on a clear slate. It is an episode in a serial story begun long before." [2] Did you ever consider that you might have been your own great grandfather or that you were that strange ancestor you have heard stories about? Perhaps your best friend in this life was your brother or sister in your last life or was a romantic partner in some long ago era.

Often the people of a particular place or a particular era reincarnate together, as evidence indicates that the people of Atlantis reincarnated many years later as a group to the United States.

Cayce helped people to understand that their actions in past lives had much to do with their present conditions and, more importantly, that they could pay off their karmic debt by forgiving themselves for what they had done to others in former lifetimes.

Perhaps some older readers will recall the work of Dr. Stevenson and others who studied the evidence for reincarnation from very specific memories of young children. Often, the children would remember their name, where they had lived and many other circumstances about a former life. And, their remembrances in many cases were able to be verified.

In more recent years there are many books giving strong evidence for reincarnation. A very prominent case discussing reincarnation was on ABC Prime time in April, 2004. It was about a boy who at the age of two began having terrible nightmares screaming about his fighter-plane on fire, he can not get out and the plane crashes. Over the next few years, the parents got more specific information. Gradually the boy gave technical information about the airplanes, naming his base, his aircraft carrier and names of his crew. The boy had three G. I. Joes and he gave them three common names (not the names a young boy would name his imaginary flying buddies.) One day after his nightmare his mother questioned him asking why did he call them by those names. His answer: They were my three friends who came to meet me when I died! It was learned later, that these were the names of his friends who had been shot down in the months just ahead of his own crash .

When the boy was four years old he told his father that he had found him and his mother because he knew they would be a good mommy and daddy. The father asked 'where' did he find them. The child said that he found them in Hawaii at the big pink hotel on the beach. His mother and father had been at the big pink hotel in Hawaii on their honeymoon a good year before his birth! This story helps to corroborate the idea that we choose our own parents, choosing them because they will give us the opportunities and /or problems we need to work out our karma.

After the episode on ABC, a group in Japan invited the boy and his family to Japan. They took them to the spot where his airplane crashed and lies submerged in very deep water in the harbor of the island. The boy saluted his former self and said goodbye.

The boy's father had tried desperately to find some explanation other than reincarnation for the stories that his son was repeating. The boy's mother early on accepted the idea that their son's revelations meant that he was, indeed, remembering a past life, but his father could not. He did not want to believe that it could have anything to do with a former life. He was a devout Christian and found it almost impossible to accept that his son or anybody else had ever lived more than once. Finally, however, he did accept the fact that the stories his son had spoken about had no other explanation than reincarnation.

I understand that there are readers objecting, objecting to the whole idea of reincarnation, some questioning on the basis of religious training, while others just find the whole concept improbable. But let us continue.

Voltaire, who did not believe in the teachings of the Church but certainly was no atheist as generally believed, asked of skeptics whether it would be more difficult to be born a second time than to be born once. Is it any more preposterous, he asked, to believe that we have lived before birth than to believe that we will live after death? Can we truly explain the miracle of birth? Can we truly explain the miracle of life after death ?

Historically, it is difficult to find a name among the famous who did not believe in life before birth as well as life after death: Plato, Aristotle, Caesar, Shakespeare, Milton, Benjamin Franklin, Ralph Waldo Emerson, Walt Whitman, Thomas Edison, Luther Burbank, George Bernard Shaw, Rudolf Steiner, Henry Ford, Rudyard Kipling, Mahatma Gandhi, Sir Winston Churchill and Charles Lindbergh, to name a few who believed and wrote about reincarnation.

ONE MORE NAME

To that list, let me add one more name – JESUS

Adding the name of Jesus to those who understood and taught reincarnation may be surprising to you, it may even be inconceivable to many readers. But for those who are well acquainted with the historical period in which Jesus lived and are aware of the philosophical understanding of the religious communities of the Holy Land of those days, it is not surprising at all. Serious students of that part of the world and of that historical era will recall that especially the Essenes, the cultural and religious group from which Jesus came, were fully conversant with the idea of many lives on the earthly plane.

Before we look at the words of Jesus on the subject, let us take a brief look at the concept of reincarnation in Judaism. The Old Testament neither denies nor proclaims rebirth of the soul, but in the Judaic tradition there is a strong indication of belief in the idea of a soul making many trips to this world before acquiring the perfection and experience to go on. The tradition teaches that Adam became, in turn, Seth, Noah, Abraham and Moses. We could include many pages to show the acceptance and understanding of reincarnation among the Jews, but to briefly demonstrate this, we will quote the Hasidic teacher Rabbi Schneur Azknabm who wrote the following "Prayer Before Retiring at Night."

> "Master of the universe! I hereby forgive any-one who has angered or vexed me, or sinned against me, either physically or financially against my honor or anything else that is mine, whether accidentally or intentionally, inadvertently or deliberately, by speech or by deed, in this incarnation or in any other," [3]

The Old Testament ended with the prophecy, "Look, I will send you the prophet Elijah before the great and terrible day the Lord comes." (Malachi 4:5). Then, in the New Testament, Matthew 16:13-14 relates that when Jesus came into the coasts of Caesarea, he indicated that belief in reincarnation was understood and accepted by his contemporaries by asking his disciples, "Whom do men say that I, the Son of Man, am?" His disciples replied, "Some say that thou art John the Baptist, some, Elias, and others Jeremiah, or one of the prophets."

Then further along in Matthew (17: 9-13) as they came down from the mountain, Jesus tells his disciples that Elijah has been reincarnated into a new body, that of John the Baptist. "Tell the vision to no man, until the Son of Man be risen again from the dead." His disciples asked him, "Why then say the scribes that Elias must first come?" and Jesus answered, "Elias truly shall first come, and restore all things. But I say unto you that Elias is already come, and they know him not, but have done unto him what they willed. Likewise shall also the Son of Man suffer of them." Then the disciples understood that he spoke unto them of John the Baptist.

This was stated even more emphatically by Jesus in Matthew 11:13-15: "For all the prophets and the Law foretold things to come until John appeared, and John is the destined Elijah, if you will but accept it. If you have ears, then hear." On another occasion (John 9:1-3) the disciples asked Jesus, "Master, who did sin, this man, or his parents that he must be born blind?" Obviously, if it were due to the man's sins, he must have sinned before he was born!

It is easy for a student of the scriptures to see that many of the Jews of Jesus's day understood and accepted the concept of reincarnation of the soul. Flavius Josephus, the famous Jewish historian of the first century, wrote of his belief in reincarnation while Origen of Alexandria (A.D. 185-254) claimed that Jesus had given his disciples the truth of reincarnation and those teachings were passed on through the apostles. He wrote, "The soul has neither beginning nor end . . .. (souls) come into this world strengthened by the victories or weakened by the defeats of their previous lives." [4]

It is clear from the scriptures that Jesus took for granted the idea of reincarnation. For example, in Mark 10: 29-31 Jesus speaks of more than one earthly life:

> "There is no man that have left house, or brethren or sisters or father, or mother . .. for my sake, and the gospel's. But he shall receive an hundredfold now in this time, houses, and brethren, and sisters, and mothers, and children, and lands, with persecutions; and in the world to come eternal life. But many that are first shall be last; and the last, first."

Biblical scholars, making the above quotation more easily under-stood, translate it to say, "But many that are first in this incarnation, shall be last or in lowly positions in the next rebirth while the last or least esteemed may be first in their future life."

Many of the secret teachings of Jesus given to his disciples were recorded in early writings. Some of these texts were called the Gnostic Gospels, based on the Greek word "gnosis" meaning "knowledge." Until being declared heretical and sought out and destroyed, these texts were considered of equal worth and of equal truth alongside the New Testament texts with which we are famil-iar. A copy of these Gnostic writings was buried in Upper Egypt by Coptic Christians to save them from the book-burning by the priests. In 1945 a peasant, while digging in his fields, discovered a large earthenware pot containing ancient papyrus texts (the Nag Hammadi Scrolls), which have proven to be the long-lost and long-sought after Gnostic Gospels.

In 365 A.D., at the Council of Nicea, which was under the control of Emperor Constantine, the "dangerous" concepts of Gnosticism, including the belief of reincarnation, were no longer accepted as dogma. Finally, in the year 553 A.D., at the Fifth Ecumenical Coun-cil, these "dangerous" truths were declared anathema and expunged from the scriptures. It was largely a political decision. The Western Roman Empire was already in complete collapse, and it was becom-ing increasingly difficult to hold back the barbarians to the east. The Eastern Empire could not tolerate any further dissension in its midst. The leaders of the Empire as well as of the Church needed to have a hell, a heaven, and a judgment day to create an atmosphere of fear and submission in order to maintain their control. The Gnostic ideas of the divinity of man, equality of women within the church, reincarnation, etc., threatened the order of the state and supremacy of the Church. Thus, religious dogmas, rules and rituals were more firmly enforced to maintain their sure control of the masses.

Later, in the late Middle Ages, the Church found it necessary once again to deal with the issue of reincarnation. This time it was the Cathar Christians of northern Italy and southern France that were the source of the problem. The Cathars insisted on teaching the earlier accepted doctrine of reincarnation. The Roman Church answered the challenge with the Inquisition in 1184 A.D. The Church, using the flaming torch of the newly formed anti-heretical organization led by the Jesuits, killed hundred of thousands of their fellow Christians under the pretext of saving the souls of those heretics who believed in that "diabolical and dangerous" doctrine. The Church leaders rightly realized that if they didn't eliminate the "heresy" of the belief in reincarnation, they would lose their power over the people. The priesthood would lose its usefulness if such a "heresy" were allowed to flourish. The entire future of the Church was at stake.

Now we are in the early years of the 21st century and it seems that the forces of religion have changed little, but I believe that we are on the verge of living to see monumental changes in all facets of society including changes in our spiritual understanding.

We should add to the evidence of reincarnation, by considering near death experiences (NDE'S). A website, Near-Death.com, lists a great number of near-death experiences of persons who "died" and were later resuscitated. Those who had the NDE'S reported going through a tunnel toward a bright light and seeing their departed family, friends and lovers waiting for them. However, they are told that they still have something to do on earth and must go back. At that moment they come back to their body. Those who have had this experience say that they no longer fear death.

In a series of books called The Law of One which were allegedly given telepathically by extraterrestrials in 1981, David Wilcock writes that "We are told that we are all perfect, holographic reflections of the One infinite Creator: That we incarnated to work on spiritual lessons and will eventually return to our original identity." [4]

Finally, let us end this chapter with some words of Jesus said to Andrew, the first- chosen of the twelve disciples and the younger brother of Peter. The words are related by Charles Lehman, who, as a child asked his parents to call him Andrew instead of his given name of Charles. As an adult he began remembering his past life as Andrew, the disciple of Jesus. The whole story is found in *The Book Of Andrew*, published November 1, 2013. The words of Jesus:

> "No one may master the lessons of Heaven in a single life, but God, a loving Father, does not decree for His children the fire of eternal damnation. Rather, He repeats his lessons with patience beyond the understanding of men, giving His children all the time they need to learn. This is why I say to you, you must be born again. Time after time you will be born of the flesh, but when, after many lives, you have learned the lessons of Heaven, you will be born of the Spirit. From that time on, eternal Paradise is yours." [5]

1. David Wilcock, *The Synchronicity Key*, p. 138.
2. Gina Cerminara, *Many Mansions*, p. 123.
3. Rabbi Shneur Azlman, quoted in Sylvia Cranston and Corey Williams, *A New Horizon in Science, Religion and Society*, p. 193.
4. David Wilcock, *The Source Field Investigations*, p. 463.
5. Charles Lehman, *The Book of Andrew*, p. 73.

❈

" Since everything is a reflection of our minds . . .
anything can be changed by our minds."
–Buddha

"I am responsible for what I see. I choose the
feelings I experience and I decide upon the goal
I would choose. And everything that seems to
happen to me, I ask for, and receive as I have
asked."
–Seth

To Hell With Hell

Chapter 7: Do We Create Our Reality?

Our life is what our thoughts make it."
–Marcus Aurelius

Do you believe that you alone are responsible for your life - your good days, your bad days? Do you take credit for your successes but blame God, the devil, or someone or something else for your failures? Does everything happen as it does because we have wished (created) it so? Are there no accidents? Our world is in conflict. It always has been. Could our change in our thinking change the world? Consider this:

> ". . . conflict in the world is the result of con-
> flict within us. We project that feeling into the
> world because we are not ready to accept that
> we are the cause, and therefore the solution,
> to the conflict. Thus wars have raged in the
> world since the beginning of time, because we
> are not ready to deal with the conflict where
> it really is – within us." [1]

Later, we will look at the Global Consciousness Project and see how people in groups really are changing the consciousness of the world, and how each of us, individually, can help to do so. But, if the conflict is within us, within our thoughts, then it seems that we should first understand something about our thinking processes so that we can work to change our thoughts. Some of what follows will be a bit dull and pedantic, but please stay with it for a bit.

A printed page only transmits information – it does not actually contain information. In like manner physical objects in our environment are not reality – they only represent, or are symbols of, reality. So we can say that our physical reality is just a language similar to the words on a printed page. Objects only have validity in our physical reality. Any object or event that we perceive is created by us. The scientific world acknowledges this. Physicist David Bohm saw that "there is a similarity between thought and matter. All matter, including ourselves, is determined 'information.' 'Information' is what determines space and time."[2] And P. D. Ouspensky claimed that "The true motion which lies at the basis of everything is the motion of thought. True energy is the energy of consciousness." [3] while physicist, Roger S. Jones writes:

> "I had come to suspect, and now felt com-
> pelled to acknowledge, that science and
> the physical world were products of human
> imagining – that we were not cool observers
> of that world, but its passionate creators."[4]

Seth, a spokesman for the paranormal viewpoint says that all events or actions are mental actions before they become physical reality. He outlines in considerable detail the process by which our thoughts and our emotions create physical matter and emphasizes the fact that we create matter just as easily with negative or violent thoughts as with thoughts of beauty or love.[5]

Physicists Bob Toben and Fred Alan Wolf came to the same conclusion as Seth, when they said that "the greater the awareness or consciousness of the observer, the greater the probability of the event occurring."[6]

To this point I believe that we have established that matter as we know it is a projection from a deeper level of consciousness and that we bring that consciousness into physical form by our thoughts and emotions. But are we willing to accept the idea that we, individually, are responsible for everything that occurs in our personal life? Are we ready to take as truth this following statement by Seth? "In each life you choose and create your own settings ... you choose your parents and whatever childhood incidents that came within your experience. You wrote the script." [7]

For those readers who feel unable or unwilling to accept the idea that each of us must take responsibility for everything that happens in our life because science indicates that it is true, or because Seth, a discarnate personality, says it to be so, let me add the following words of Jesus in which he suggests that we repeat often to ourselves:

> "I am responsible for what I see. I choose
> the feelings I experience and I decide upon
> the goal I would choose. And everything that
> seems to happen to me I ask for, and receive
> as I have asked." [8]

That, I believe, is very hard for most of us to accept easily. For myself, I often ask, if I wrote my script, why did I include such garbage, such embarrassment, such pain, such grief? When pain, difficulties, challenges, etc take place in our life (in our script), we, in our conscious self, look for something or someone to blame them on. We don't want to admit, certainly not to ourselves, that we asked for all this. Seth, too, answers that yes, indeed, we do ask for what we experience.

He says that each of us creates our individual physical reality and that en masse we create the "glories and the terrors" that take place in the experiences of our world. We create, at deep unconscious levels, every cell that makes up our physical body with great "discrimination, miraculous clarity, and intimate unconscious knowledge of each minute cell that composes it." [9]

Hopefully, when we wrote our script before coming into this physical world once again, we wrote it to show that we would change our beliefs and attitudes and, in one sense, feel that we are changing the written script.

Our ideas and our emotions are a result of our beliefs, so anything that we accept as truth is only a belief of ours and that we must tell ourselves that, just because we believe something, does not necessarily make it true. We should disregard any belief of ours that implies limitations of any kind and always keep in mind that it is our conscious beliefs that control the functioning of our bodies; and that it is not, as we have generally believed, the other way around.

In other words, we get what we think about. We experience what we concentrate upon. We attract to ourselves what we fear. If we dwell upon our supposed limitations, we will experience them. If we focus positively on our possibilities, we will accomplish them. Obviously then, if we can change our thinking we can change in very concrete ways the health of our body and all aspects of our relationships to others. En masse, we can really change the world.

Years ago, while teaching ancient and modern world history at Horace Mann School in New York City, I spent four weekends taking the Silva Mind Control course. Silva Mind suggests that we start each day saying to ourselves, "Every day, in every way, I am getting better and better." So, when a friend asks us how we are, he or she does not, in most cases, want a litany of our problems and pains. A good answer might be, "better and better".

The book, *Conversations with God*, which deals at length with the subject of creating our own reality has this to say:

> "'I am' is the strongest creative statement in
> the universe. Whatever you think, whatever
> you say, following the words 'I am', sets into
> motion those experiences, calls them forth,
> brings them to you. . . The universe responds

to 'I am' as would a genie in a bottle. "[10]

THE GLOBAL CONSCIOUSNESS PROJECT

The Global Consciousness Project began in 1979. It was begun with the desire to determine if our human minds, especially in large groups, can cause effects or changes in the consciousness of the public that would be measurable. After much study they learned that the strongest effects were found to take place when people got together for a purpose or in ritual or in response to a global happening.

After many studies giving very positive results, they found that during and after the 9/11 attack in NYC the effects were exceptionally strong. It was found that the effects were stronger the closer a person was to NYC.

Three days after 9/11 there was a worldwide prayer for peace. Millions throughout the world took part in meditation and periods of silence. Again the instruments recorded a strong response throughout the world.

When Obama was elected in 2008, the measuring instruments showed equal strong results to the peace meditations after 9/11 and dozens of continuing studies have shown similar strong positive effects.

As a close to this chapter I would like to use the words of David Wilcock speaking of the Global Consciousness project:

> 'Thanks to the Global Consciousness Project, we now have compelling evidence that our own minds can also create a direct, measurable effect on how electricity flows throughout the wires, components and computer chips all over the world. It appears that in moments of great tragedy, or times when many of us focus on the same event, our minds create worldwide hiccups in the flow of energy. Our thoughts do seem to create

an energy that directly affects the behavior of others." [11]

1. James Twyman, quoted in David Wilcock, *The Source Field Invesigations*, p. 24.
2. David Bohm, quoted in Gary Zukov, *The Dancing Wu Li Masters: An Overview of the New Physics*, p. 327.
3. P. D. Ouspensky, quoted in Michael Friedman, *Bridging Science and Spirit*, p. 133.
4. Roger S. Jones, *Physics as Metaphor*, p. 3.
5. Jane Roberts, *Seth Speaks: The Eternal Validity of the Soul*, pp. 75-76.
6. Bob Toben and Fred Alan Wolfe, *Space, Time and Beyond*, p. 130.
7. Jane Roberts, *op. cit.*, p 11.
8. *A Course in Miracles, Text*, p. 448.
9. Jane Roberts, *op. cit.*, pp. 10-11.
10. Neale Donald Walsch, *Conversations with God, Book 1*, p. 93.
11. David Wilcock, *The Source Field Investigations*, p. 242.

※

*"Time is not at all what it seems. It does not
flow in only one direction, and the future exists
simultaneously with the past."*
–Einstein

*"Time is what prevents everything from happening
at once."*
–John Wheeler

*"And all of time is but the mad belief that what is
over is still here and now."*
–Gary Reynard

*"The future is any past memory that is still potent
enough to impulse your behavior now.*
–Barbara Hand Clow

Chapter 8: Time

*Eternity is not everlasting time but a moment
without time. Hence, being timeless, all of eternity
is wholly and completely present right NOW."*
–Ken Wilber

What is time? In trying to give an answer, I think most of us
would agree with St. Augustine's reply when he was asked the
question. He answered by saying, "If no one asks me, I know what
it is. If I wish to explain it to him who asks me I do not know." [1]

Is time just an illusion?

Time appears to us to be linear. Living "in time" we perceive
and experience a past, a present and a future. In the real reality,
time is holographic in the sense that all of time is contained in the
original instant of creation. If we were still aware of our Oneness
and the "little ripple" or "tiny mad idea" had never happened we
would not experience time or space. "To the eye of eternity, there
is no "then", either past or present." [2]

From the physicist's point of view, time is just one dimension of
a multi-dimensional reality. The whole concept of time is a result of

the process of projection from the implicate order into the explicate order. That is, from the transcendental realm outside of space and time into our physical three-dimensional realm. In the transcendent realm (the implicate) there is no need for time as all events are inter-connected instantly. When consciousness "chooses" an event or object to be explicated or projected into our physical universe, time is defined – time being the succession of such projections. So, in a sense we can say that matter creates both time and space.

Seth, giving the paranormal explanation, says the same, that time is just one dimension of a multi-dimensional reality:

> "What separates events is not time, but your perception. You perceive events one-at-a-time. Time as it appears to you is, instead, a psychic organization of experience. The seeming beginning and end of an event; the seeming birth and death, are simply other dimensions of experience as, for example, height, width, depth." [3]

And as the science writers of *The View from the Center of the Universe* define the idea, "There is no direction to time, and every time is the same as every other," [4] and "Much of our future already exists – it just hasn't gotten here yet . . . in some sense the past of the universe lies in our future." [5]

And combining space and time, they write, "Before the Big Bang there was no preexisting space . . . The Big Bang happened everywhere. It created the possibility of both 'where ' and 'when', all wheres and whens are inside the Big Bang." [6]

The role of time is understood better when we consider the plan of the ego to convince each of us (the Sons of God) not to remember our true identity. Time becomes the trap that tricks us into believing that reality is what it appears to be. "The instant the idea of separation entered the mind of God's Son, in that same instant was God's answer given (see Chapter *The Holy Spirit*). In time this happened very long ago. In reality it never happened at all." [7]

It is often suggested that we should think of time as a vertical concept instead of as a horizontal or linear concept – to think of all the pages of time being on a spindle in one vertical stack, each page or moment of time existing simultaneously. "There is only One moment – this moment – the Eternal Moment of Now." [8]

Einstein's theory of relativity showed us that time and space are relative to each other, that space and time are a continuum. Scientists now add to his statement, saying that everything is part of that continuum. Everything is One!

Did Time Stand Still?

Was there a "slip in time" on a National Airlines 727 while landing at Miami International Airport? [9] The flight crew had just been given final landing instructions from the tower. Suddenly the image of the plane disappeared from the radar screens. Emergency crews were alerted, looking for a crash or flight diversion of some kind. Nothing! Other planes continued to fly through the space that that flight had been in and continued to land. Everything was normal except that that plane was just missing.

Suddenly, ten minutes later, the image of that flight re-appeared on the control tower's screen, appearing exactly at the same location it had been when it disappeared. The plane landed, a perfect normal landing. Emergency crews rushed to the plane. The flight crew was startled by all the excited questions, demanding to learn what had happened, "where were you? You did not exist for ten minutes!" The crew simply stated that everything was normal, the tower had given them final landing instructions and they landed. Period. Nothing unusual. The watches of all the crew members, and of the passengers were ten minutes late.

It should probably be noted that this occurred in Florida, close to the Bermuda Triangle where hundreds of other unanswered flight irregularities have happened.

1. Joel R. Primack & Nancy Ellen Abrams, *The View From the Center of the Universe*, p. 23.
2. Ken Wilber, *Eye to Eye*, p. 298.
3. Jane Roberts, *Seth Speaks*, p. 372.
4. Joel R. Primack and Nancy Ellen Abrams, *op. cit.*, p. 192.
5. *Ibid.*, p. 141.
6. *Ibid.*, p. 124.
7. *A Course in Miracles, Manual*, p. 5.
8. Neale Donald Walsch. *Conversations With God, Book II*, p. 29.

"The world is set up to undergo the biggest expansion in history."
–Gary Renard

"You are ready to graduate from a history of fear into a future of love and if you want your diplomas, you must now stretch your minds right out of your skulls."
–Barbara Hand Clow

Chapter 9: A New Golden Age

"You are on the verge of a creative renaissance
that will be like a supernova."
–Barbara Hand Clow

Are we entering a new age, a NEW Golden Age? Looking out at the world in this year of 2014 as I am writing these words, there seems to be little to make us optimistic. On the other hand, there are many indications that it just might be true that a new and better world is waiting for us on tomorrow's horizon. Earlier when we talked about the evolution of man, we concluded that we did not evolve in slow evolutionary changes (Darwinian Evolution) as there is no evidence to support that belief. Now the latest findings and conclusions of the world of anthropologists, paleontologists and other scientific fields show that man has developed in spurts – sudden spurts occurring approximately every 26,000 years. To set the scene for our discussion, let us begin with this:

> "Our earth is only four billion years old, and
> it very likely started out as a molten rock.
> Things didn't cool down enough for oceans
> to form until 3.8 billion years ago. But even

at this time, rock samples have been found
that contain all the basic isotopes plants create
from photosynthesis. Even better, a primitive,
yeast-like organism has also been found in
3.8 billion-year-old rocks. That means that as
soon as the earth had water, life essentially
appeared instantaneously." [1]

Fossil microbes found in rocks of 3.5 billion years ago are just
like the organisms of today and are "just as complex. Life may be
improbable, but it was quick." [2] An MIT biologist calculated to see
how likely it could be that one protein could form by chance and
his calculation showed only one chance in a number with sixty-five
zeroes!

David Wilcock, discussing the very latest of physicist's findings
(August, 2013), says there is now proof for the idea that evolution
could be completely spontaneous and would require nothing more
than to rearrange the DNA molecules of an existing species. [3]

These concepts help to make the idea that evolution has occurred
in sudden bursts more understandable. The records show that sudden bursts of creativity have occurred approximately every 26,000
years in synchronicity with the precession of the equinoxes. We are
now leaving the Age of Pisces and entering the Age of Aquarius. It
is more than a coincidence to note that the Mayans had calculated
the same year of the calendar to end one age and to begin another.
The words of David Wilcock puts these ideas together:

"Our own solar system appears to be moving
into an area of greater coherence – which is
creating a short-term, rapid evolution of human DNA and consciousness . . . The Maya
calendar end-date, the expected arrival date
for the Age of Aquarius and the exact time
window for the coming Golden Age in Hindu
scriptures all highlight the same, small win-

dow of time – circa 2012 – as a key watermark for when these changes will occur. Humans gained a massive burst of intelligence fifty thousand years ago, and the Neanderthals phased out of the evolutionary cycle some twenty-five thousand years ago – right on schedule with the end of each Great Year. Our DNA has been evolving one hundred times faster in the last five thousand years than in all human history." [4]

The Neanderthals went extinct in the sudden changes of approximately 25, 000 years ago, when we moved from the age of Aries to the Age of Pisces. Going back another 25,000 years to approximately 50,000 years ago,moving from the Age of Taurus to the Age of Aries we find that there was a sudden big advancement in Man's development. For the first time we began using sophisticated tools, made musical instruments, artistic drawings and beaded jewelry. Also, it should be noted that it was 50,000 years ago when there was a sudden mass extinction of the world's giant mammals. (It was about 65 million years ago when the dinosaurs became extinct).

It is now late 2013 as I write these words. The Mayan Calendar has just reached its end date of Dec., 2012, and we are now entering the Age of Aquarius. I believe that many readers feel (with a "knowingness") that we are on the verge of something new, something wonderful beyond man's expectations.

Barbara Hand Clow says, "You are on the verge of a creative renaissance that will be like a supernova," [5] while David Wilcock puts it this way: " Life on earth will transition into a far more powerful, harmonious and evolved level as we move into the Age of Aquarius." [6]

Take out a dollar bill. Look at the pyramid on the Great Seal of the United States. The date at the bottom of the pyramid is 1776, the date of the foundation of our government. The flat top of the pyramid brings us to 2,012 . Counting the eye, brings us to 2,032.

Keep this in mind as you look Inside the dome of the Capitol at the painting called "The Apotheosis of Washington", showing Washington having been transformed into a divine state. Also, you will see inside the dome is a frieze with the Aztec Calendar ending in 2012.

Did the founders of our nation know something? Was America founded to fulfill the ancient prophecies of a new Golden Age to begin after the Year 2012? David Wilcock has some interesting thoughts:

> "The very essence of the science and prophecies .. . show that the change we are going through is woven directly into our DNA... . . The United States may have been intended to pave the way for this transformation, . . . but ultimately it is the galaxy, the Sun and earth itself that are directing this evolutionary process, as well as various relatives we appear to have." [7]

OUR ALIEN FRIENDS

Who are those various relatives we appear to have in the above quotation? Are they not our alien friends? I believe that we are ready to be told the truth about the aliens among us. They, our friends, are here working with our military to keep us safe.

Some readers will remember what Jimmy Carter said when he was running for the presidency. He had had a personal UFO sighting in Oct. of 1969. His words: "If I become president, I'll make every piece of information this country has about UFO sightings available to the public and the scientists." [8] He never said a word about it after his election. I do not think we need to ask why.

On May 10, 2010, there was an Executive Summary Briefing in which testimony described over 50 different varieties of extraterrestrial life of human appearance that are cooperating with our military.

"UFO's, apparently piloted by benevolent extraterrestrial humans, have consistently interfered with the nuclear arsenals of every country that possesses them – not to attack us, but rather to prevent any political faction from destroying the planet," [9]

President Eisenhower, supposedly missing from the White House for three days, was reported to have been at an Air Force Base in Southern California. At the time there was wild speculation that he was meeting with aliens that offered him the secrets of inter-galactic travel if he would destroy all our atomic weapons. Allegedly he refused, worried that Russia would destroy us if we could not retaliate.

On Sept. 27, 2010 at the UFO-Nukes Connection press conference, seven US Air Force veterans gave their eyewitness testimony of incursions by UFOs during the days of the Cold War. Just a few days later, on October 2, a UFO over the air base in Cheyenne, Wyoming powered down fifty Minuteman III missiles and they remained down for 26 hours. [10]

It is expected by many that there will be a mass worldwide landing of UFOs in our not-too-distant future. Many on earth will think it to be an invasion, but the ET's will assure the world that it is a very positive event for us.

". . . there will be miracles the like of which have never before been seen. We will come with an armada of spaceships, glistening in the morning light, prepared to do whatever is necessary to protect you from any and all hardships." [11]

Barbara Marciniak, a renowned author who writes about our ancient beginnings wrote in 2004:

"A so-called official acknowledgement of the
presence of intelligent life-forms that share
time and space with you is just around the
corner. . . A full acknowledgment of the extraterrestrial presence will unravel society's
traditional religious beliefs concerning your
origins. Your heritage is from the stars, and
understanding the multi-layered complexities
of this truth is of premier importance to the
spiritual transformation of humanity." [12]

There are a great number of other interesting and tantalizing
predictions for the years of the not-too-distant future. Some of them
may seem improbable or even impossible. But as I remember when
returning home from the Air Corps in 1946, my father talked about
how impossible and crazy was all the talk about the possibility of
television. Then a few years later, returning home again from my
home in NYC, my mother and father were sitting in front of a television and thinking it perfectly normal.

Before listing a few predictions and to stimulate your optimism
and your expectations for the years ahead, consider these words:

"Humanity is rapidly approaching the edge
of the great cosmic cliffs of consciousness.
What you do now, the choices you make, will
determine a course of experience more complex and astounding than you can currently
imagine. The dawning of a new revolution in
consciousness is at hand. [14]

So, let's look at a few predictions – from different sources,
sources which I consider credible:

New York to California by commercial air
travel in thirty minutes.

Dow Jones average will be 100,000 by mid-century.
Man will walk on Mars and find evidence showing that at one time intelligent life existed there.
Quantum computers beyond our wildest dreams.
Tourist trips to the moon.
Teleportation. By the end of the century we will be able to be beamed to the moon in three seconds.

Some of these predictions may seem "far-out thinking", but we should remember that just a few years ago it was "far-out thinking" that man would walk on the moon.

That short list of predictions for the future sound like fun and games, but unfortunately it seems we will still be our usual human selves and continue with our personal animosities and our international problems and even war, at least as long as we are suffering the birth pangs of our entrance into the new Golden Age. There is the prediction that in the early years of the New Age, at least one western or western orbit city will be destroyed by an atomic weapon after which the USA will destroy the capital city of the guilty nation and peace will follow.

But looking beyond predictions, let us with optimism look ahead to a world where we will have more love and empathy for all nations and all peoples, a world where we will learn to understand that we, indeed, are ONE

"Once we finally decide not to discriminate against one another, and to strive for a better world, peace and freedom will be ours for the taking – and we will enter into an unprecedented Golden Age." [15]

1. David Wilcock, *The Source Field Investigations*, p. 187.
2. *Ibid.*
3. *Ibid.*, p. 209.
4. *Ibid.*, p. 214.
5. Barbara Hand Clow, *The Pleiadian Agenda*, p. 102.
6. David Wilcock, *The Synchronicity Key*, p. 380.
7. David Wilcock, *The Source Field Investigations*, p. 429.
8. Jimmy Carter, quoted in David Wilcock, *The Synchronicity Key*. p. 331.
9. David Wilcock, *The Source Field Investigations*, p.440.
10. David wilcock, *The Synchronicity Key*, p. 316.
11. *Ibid.*, p. 370.
12. Barbara Marciniak, *The Path of Empowerment*, p. .246.
13. David Wilcock, *The Synchronicity Key*, p. 453.
14. Barbara Marciniak, *op. cit.*, p. 2.
15. David Wilcock, *The Synchronicity Key*, p.304.

❧

Who created the universe?
You did!
And
when you finally remember who you are,
Your creation, the universe
will disappear
because
it never really was!

You are everything,
every being, every emotion
every event, every situation.
You are unity. You are infinity.
You are love/light, light/love.
You are.
This is the law of one.
Law Of Love

Part II

Introduction To Part II

Perhaps some readers after reading Part I are still unconvinced that there is no Hell. Here in Part II we are going to talk about WHO YOU REALLY ARE. When you really understand who you are, the idea of a hell will be unthinkable. The idea of any punishment after your earthly lives would never enter your mind. To get you into a thinking frame of mind about who you are, pause for a few moments and consider these quotations from Ken Wilber:

> "Show me the Self you had before the Big Bang, and I will show you the Spirit of the entire Kosmos. And as for that pure, timeless. formless Spirit:
> You ... Are ... That. (1)

> "Don't you remember who and what you really are? Did not even Saint Clement say, He who knows himself knows God." (2)

So, onto the chapters of part II. Please read them with a quiet thoughtful mind and be prepared to meet ideas which may be very different from what you have been taught in your religious upbringing.

1. Ken Wilber., *The Simple Feeling of Being*, Shambhala Publications, 300 Massachusetts Avenue, Boston, Mass., p. 5
2. Ibid, P. 2 .

Chapter 10: The Nature of God and the Nature of Man

" Who is God?" "What is God?"
"I reply: Isness,
Isness is God."
—Meister Eckhart (1260 - 1329)

The Christian minister pronounces the benediction: "The Lord lift up His countenance upon thee, and give thee peace." When we listen to those words, what image do we have in our mind's eye? How do we visualize God? I suspect that most of us visualize a being in the image of man; perhaps an imposing Moses-like figure with a long beard, looking down upon us most benevolently. However, earlier in the sermon when the minister was preaching about a hell awaiting us, we probably pictured a God of wrath ready to throw us into a pit of fire. Both of these mental pictures of God are very much that of a human figure, not too different from ourselves.

The Greeks, Romans and earlier peoples had what we have patronizingly called anthropomorphic gods. Do we not also make our God into the likeness of Man? Does not the benediction quoted above picture an anthropomorphic God? Does not the typical Christian minister threaten his listeners with a God showing all the attributes of humans?

In the Old Testament we read of a god who had all the worst attributes of man. He was a god of war, a jealous god, a god of no mercy who exhibited rage, hate and vengeance. He was racist, homophobic, showed favoritism and demeaned women. Do we really believe that our Creator God has such attributes? When we seriously contemplate God I believe that most readers fully realize that God is not a superhuman, but is pure Spirit and does not have a body or in any way can anthropomorphic traits be attributed to Him.

Does it not then follow that we cannot but fail in any attempt to define God. After all, He created us in His image, but, unfortunately we made Him in our image. The nature of God cannot possibly be known by us in our ego self, believing ourselves to be separate from Him and limited in our understanding by the constraints of our physical and psychological dimensions. When we leave those constraints behind and return to the awareness of who we really are, we will better understand what God is, for then we will be at One with Him finding ourselves an extension of His very being. We are speaking here about the real me, the real you – not of our physical bodies.

God is the Unmoved Mover, the First Cause, the Creator of All That Is. Jesus says, "We say 'God is' and then we cease to speak, for in that knowledge words are meaningless." [1] Meister Eckhart's famous line says the same, "What is God? God is."

A Course in Miracles calls any attempt to define God beyond saying that God is Spirit - perfect, eternal, without form and limitless - as "senseless musings." God's basic function is extending His being in creation. God's creation, Christ, God's one Son, is the extension of His very essence. "It should be especially noted that God has only one Son. If all His creations are His Sons, every one must be an integral part of the whole Sonship. The Sonship in its oneness transcends the sum of its parts." [2].

In Christianity, God's only-begotten Son is identified as exclusively Jesus, but as we have attempted to show throughout this work, each one of us is His "only-begotten Son ." Jesus said that he is not different from us or in any way separate from us except in "time". "The name of Jesus is the name of one who was a man but saw the face of Christ in all his brothers and remembered God. So he became identified with Christ, a man no longer, but at one with God. . . Is he the Christ? Oh yes along with you," [3]

Man is at Home with God, partaking of the is-ness of God, never having left Heaven (that state of awareness of being at One with God). So in the true reality, we are One with Him but we are not the Creator. Many people who call themselves New Agers like to say, "I am God." But they should remember that God created us, His Sons and Daughters. We did not create Him. We are not in a reciprocal relation with our Creator. This becomes more clear if we think of our physical self as the child of our parents. Our parents created us, we did not create them.

The only part of us humans that is real and eternal is Spirit. This is the only part of us that God created. Our body is just the illusionary physical vehicle that we are carrying around in this dream existence. It is our vehicle which we use for experiencing until we come to finally realize that there must be more than this and return to an understanding of who we really are. In our ego driven body we have what Ken Wapnick [X], perhaps the world's principal spokesman for a clear understanding of *A course in Miracles*, calls the "unholy trinity of sin guilt and fear." [4]

This "unholy trinity" basically delineates the nature of us living in a physical body, the nature of the "separated man." Recall our "tiny mad idea", thinking that it may be nice to go out on our own and create like our Father. Then, because of the awful guilt that followed, we created the universe as a place where we thought we could hide from our Creator. We Feared that the One who created us out of His very essence of love was going to destroy us in an act of vengeance. So, we created our various religions to heal our broken relationship with God. But as history has shown us, our religions have unfortunately perpetuated the insane beliefs of sin, guilt and fear. Our ego loves all this. The ego uses the "unholy trinity" to control us and to keep us from remembering our true relationship with God.

We have spoken of the "unholy trinity" of sin, guilt and fear. Now, let us speak of the "Holy Trinity". God our Creator, is a holy Triune Being: God the Father, God the Son and God the Holy Spirit. Neale Donald Walsch has an interesting way of saying this: God the Father is knowing, the parent of all understanding and of experience; God the Son is experiencing, the acting out of what the Father knows of itself; God the Holy Spirit is being, the exquisite is-ness through the memory of both the knowing and experiencing."[5]

One might say that the signature of God is His triune nature. This triune nature or aspect repeats itself throughout all of the higher realms of reality: Subconscious, conscious, superconscious; mind, body, spirit; thought, word, deed; energy, matter, antimatter; mind, heart, soul. Even when speaking of time and space there is a past, present and future and a here, there and in-between. Only in matters of our physical three-dimensional gross relationships do we have a dual relationship instead of a triune relationship. We have opposites: up-down, hot-cold, fast-slow, male-female etc., which we have discussed earlier. But opposites are only seen as opposites by us while in this manifested physical reality. These perceived opposites are really part of a deep unity which we cannot comprehend.

To summarize, then, in speaking of the nature of man, I think that we can say that we are not sinful and do not need to experience guilt and the subsequent fear of a vengeful God. God is pure unconditional Love and to repeat what has been said before, there are only two basic emotions - love and fear. And since love is all encompassing there can be no opposite, there can be no fear .. Love is all there is.

We are boastful when, like many do, we claim to have a sinful nature, when we, in effect, put on sack cloths and ashes to demonstrate our degradation before God and man. We are arrogant when we claim to know more than God. God says that we are sinless, perfect and eternal. Who are we to confound the words of our Creator? On this subject Ken Wilber has some powerful words:

"The radical secret of the supreme identity is that there is only God. There is only the Kosmos of One Taste, always already perfectly accomplished, always already the sound of one hand clapping. And the very belief that we could deviate from this is itself the utter arrogance of the egoic delusion, the haunting mask of divine egoism floating over the smoking ruins of its own contracting tendencies. [6]

1. *A Course In Miracles, Workbook*, p. 32.
2. *A Course in Miracles, Text*. p. 33.
3. *A Course In Miracles, Manual*. p. 87.
4. Kenneth Wapnick, *Love Does Not Condemn*, p. 439.
5. Neale Donald Walsch, *Conversations With God, Book I*, p. 30.
6. Ken Wilber, *A Brief History of Everything*, p. 305.

Chapter 11: Jesus

Is He the Christ? O yes, along with you.
–A Course in Miracles

Jesus Christ. As unbelievable as it may seem to most readers, there are many Christians who think that "Christ" is the last name of Jesus! Most of my readers, I'm sure are aware that "Christ" is a title. It is correctly "Jesus, the Christ" or "The Christ Jesus." This idea is expressed clearly in the following passage in *A Course In Miracles*.

> "The name of Jesus is the name of one who was a man but saw the face of Christ in all his brothers and remembered God. So he became identified with Christ, a man no longer but at one with God . . . Jesus remains a savior because he saw the false without accepting it as true. And Christ needed his form (the physical body) that he might appear to men and save them from their own illusions." [1]

Jesus is our elder brother, our way-shower, the light upon our path. Yes I believe that, but I do not believe he wanted us to make an idol of him or to worship him. I believe that he came to teach us to become aware of our own divinity, to help us to realize that we are all God's Sons and Daughters. I do not believe that he intended to start a new religion, to institute a set of rules or to introduce ritualistic practices in his name. Did not Jesus tell us that we would not only equal his miracles but to do even greater things than he had done?

Jesus was no different from the rest of mankind, no different from you and me, except in time. The entity Jesus went through the illusion of separateness from his Father as we all have, but was the first to fully awake from that illusion. He was the first to fully realize his complete identity with Christ. "In the beginning was the Word. . . and the Word was with God and the Word was God. . . and the Word was made flesh and dwelt among us." (St.. John 1:1, 14)

Virgin Birth?

Was Jesus born of a virgin? The virgin birth of Jesus is perhaps the most sacred belief in Christendom. To even question this belief is considered sacrilege to most Christians. For most of my early years I accepted the teaching of the virgin birth but now I no longer accept that teaching, for two principle reasons.

First, a careful study of the New Testament refutes the concept. The book of I Thessalonians, was the first epistle written by Paul and was the first book written of the New Testament. It was written about twenty years after the death of Jesus. His letters to the Galatians and to the Corinthians came shortly after. In these epistles he gave not even a hint of anything other than a normal birth of Jesus. His passionate message was that Jesus was filled with the spirit of God and that we, too, should follow his example and walk with him in the Spirit. Paul's only references to the birth of Jesus were in Galatians where he wrote that Jesus was born of a woman and in Romans 1:3, where he clearly shows Joseph to be the physical father of Jesus. "Concerning his son Jesus Christ our Lord, which was made of the seed of David according to the flesh." The lineage of Jesus back to King David is from Joseph, his father, not from Mary, his mother! This lineage is traced in the first chapter of the Gospel of Matthew, chapter I, verses 1 threw 16, which ends reading, "and Jacob begat Joseph, the husband of Mary, of whom was born Jesus . . . "

In the book of Mark, the first-written of the four Gospels which occur at the beginning of the New Testament, there is no reference to an unusual birth of Jesus. It is in Matthew (the third written of the gospels) where we find the first reference to the Old Testament prophecies from which he mistranslated the reference to a "young woman" to read a "young virgin." The entire scenario of the birth of Jesus was put together by incorporating various Old Testament stories: for example, the story of Rebekah and the Song of Hannah. Even the story of the star announcing Jesus' birth was borrowed from a story in the book of Numbers.

Are the Gospels the Word of God?

As we have learned above, various writers of the gospels and of the epistles do not always agree with one another. In the Old Testament there are many errors in historical facts. The question as to whether the Bible is the very literal word of God must be faced by all, even by the fundamentalists, both Roman Catholic and Protestant. John Shelby Spong, a bishop of the Episcopal Church and a fervid lover of the Bible, has this to say:

> "The Gospels are first-century narrations based on first-century interpretations. . . One must never identify the text with the revelation or the messenger with the message. That has been the major error in our two thousand years of Christian history. It is an insight that today is still feared and resisted. But let it be clearly stated, the Gospels are not in any literal sense holy, they are not accurate

and they are not to be confused with reality.
They are rather beautiful portraits painted by
first-century Jewish artists, designed to point
the reader toward that which is in fact holy,
accurate and real." [2]

My second, and more important, reason for no longer accepting the concept of the virgin birth of Jesus is that it is exceedingly important for us that Jesus did have a normal birth. If the conception of Jesus were anything but normal, having both a physical father and a physical mother, his message to us would be entirely meaningless, would it not? He came to show us that he was a "son of man" as we all are (in our physical bodies) and that we can all become fully Christed as he became. If he had been born in some supernatural way, that would mean that we would not be able to follow his example. Jesus was the only begotten Son of God which we also are, but we have forgotten that reality. Recall that he said that the only difference between himself and us is that he knew who he was, a Son of God, and that when we come to that same awareness that each one of us is part of the Sonship of God we will do miracles equal and even greater than those he had done.

We have made a mockery of the life and teachings of Jesus. We have corrupted his message of love and forgiveness. We have allowed the religious leaders to pervert our understanding of his words. In short, we have made a new religion about, and around, the life of Jesus, but we have ignored his true teachings. We worship him instead of following in his footsteps. Ralph Waldo Emerson wrote:

"Is it not time to present this matter of
Christianity exactly as it is, to take away all
false reverence for Jesus and not mistake the
stream for the source." [3]

Thomas Jefferson, the author of the Declaration of Independence and our third president, was dismayed when he realized that the New Testament account of Jesus had been tampered with by additions, subtractions and revisions. In a letter to Dr.. Benjamin rush, he wrote:

> "To the corruption of Christianity, I am, indeed opposed but not to the genuine precepts of Jesus himself. I am a Christian in the only sense in which he wanted anyone to be: sincerely attached to his doctrines in preference to all others, ascribing himself to every human excellence; and believing he never claimed any other." [4]

I would like to close this chapter making clear that Jesus is our link back to God, back to the realization that we never left God. He is "the way, the truth and the life", the meaning of which he makes clear:

> ". . . the Holy spirit is glad when you learn from mine (experiences) and be reawakened by them. That is the only way in which I can be perceived as the way, the truth and the life." [5]

1. *A Course in Miracles, Manual*, p. 87.
2. John Shelby Spong, *Why Christianity Must Change Or Die*, pp. 107-108.
3. Steven Mitchell, *The Gospel According To Jesus*. p. 17.
4. *Ibid.*, p. 5.
5. *A Course In Miracles, Text*. p. 94.

Chapter 12: The Separation

"We have come to the dawning realization that
God might not be separated from us, but rather
deep within us."
                                    –Bishop Shelby Spong

As the reader knows, I was reared in a fundamentalist Christian home. We attended the small local Baptist Church. Readers of a similar background can attest to the great number of sermons I was subjected to that warned me of hell-fire and damnation because of what Adam and Eve had done in the Garden of Eden. Because God had driven them out of the Garden, God had turned his face away from me, and I was doomed to eternal separation from Him unless...! Unless I followed the prescribed ritual of publicly admitting my sin and asking Jesus to save me from God's wrath.

I heard those frightening sermons two (sometimes even three) times on Sunday and once during the week. A few times a year we would attend revival meetings nightly for a week or more, meetings not only in our church but in other fundamentalist churches in our town or nearby towns, or even in large tents erected on an empty village lot or in someone's pasture.

Those visiting revival preachers really knew how to scare the devil out of me. Too, they were usually from a distant city and therefore "special". Often they were advertised as ex-sinners of the worst kind. The more wicked they had been in their past, the more righteous they were said to be now, and thus worthy of our rapt attention. It seemed that those attending the meetings wanted to live vicariously the sins of the preacher.

Today Christian ministers still speak of man's separation from his Creator, but what do they really mean when they speak of separation from God? When did we become separated? Why did it happen? Where did it happen? Hey, maybe it never did happen.

Before attempting to give answers to those questions, lets first look at the historically accepted interpretation of the separation by the Christian churches, Roman Catholic and Protestant . According to that scenario Adam and Eve ate of the tree of knowledge and were expelled from Paradise (Heaven). Since then and because of that act man has been conceived and born in sin. Then, as a sinner, one has need of salvation from eternal punishment in a hell of torture by a vengeful God. The Roman Churches and various protestant groups do not see *eye to eye* on the details of salvation, but generally agree that Jesus, the only Son of God, is the savior.

Assuming just for a moment that humanity is in need of salvation and that salvation is possible only through Jesus, why, then, did God send Jesus to the Greco-Roman world of his day? Why were the people of the Roman Empire, and in particular, that rebellious corner of the Empire in Palestine, chosen for salvation and not the Chinese or the Africans or the natives of North America or even the peoples of the remote islands of the Pacific? The words of Jesus have not to this day reached some of the more inaccessible places on the planet. Are these souls then lost for ever? They are, it seems, if the historically accepted ideas of the Christian world are true.

The principal implication of the Christian idea that mankind was separated from his creator is that billions of souls are forever lost from God. Lost forever are those from the past, those living in the present and those yet to be born (including billions who never heard of Jesus or the word "Christian," or even had the chance to hear a Pat Robertson or a Billy Graham.)

But this scenario is not truly biblical. It turns the teachings of Jesus upside down. Jesus taught his disciples that when they came to the realization that they were Sons of God just as he was, they would be equal to him and do even greater miracles than he had done.

Unfortunately, there are many in our world who want to continue to insist that they are sinners – sinners "saved by the grace of god" – and then take pride in their chosen status. I recall some folk within our church circle when I was young, who acted very pious, disdained those in the community who were "sinful" – those who drank beer in the local tavern, frequented the dance halls with their loose-living friends and seemed to be happy, easygoing folks. Even in my young years I had the strong suspicion that my Christian friends had little love for these "sinning" folks because they seemed to actually enjoy life. My Christian friends were serious, sober, seldom-smiling folk, always finding fault with others and proclaiming with great satisfaction that those who sinned certainly deserved their eternity in flames with the devil. In my childish innocence, I felt more friendly and warm toward those happy, carefree "sinners" than I did toward the self-righteous churchgoers.

But it seems that we were never really separated from our Creator. Let's listen a moment to the words of Jesus.

> "To be alone is to be separated from infinity, but how can this be if infinity has no end? No one can be beyond the limitless, because what has no limits must be everywhere. There are no beginnings or endings in God, whose universe is Himself. Can you exclude yourself from God ...? I and my Father are one with you ... Do you really believe that part of God can be missing or lost to Him." [1]

Meister Eckhart, nearly seven hundred years ago said the same so beautifully and succinctly. "God is at home. It is we who have gone out for a walk," [2] And as Emmanuel says it in our time.

> "The separation from God began a journey
> of love. The individuating consciousness
> seeks to know itself fully and completely so
> that it can return to Oneness . . . The prodigal
> son returns. In truth, one never "fell" at all.
> The Fall is a symbol of human experience.
> As a symbol it is the forgetting of the initial
> purpose of individuation, getting lost in dis-
> traction, the intent of the soul forgotten. How
> could one leave God? One is God." [3]

For thousands of years we have experienced lives of toil and pain, lives of guilt, loneliness and despair, lives with the belief that God had abandoned us. We have debased ourselves and participated in all sorts of rituals, chanted innumerable liturgies and believed in differing dogmas created by the wily or unquestioning priests and self-appointed religious authorities. Millennium after millennium and century after century we have lived with the illusion of sepa- ration and desperately have sought deliverance from the bondage of sin.

Then Jesus came. Two thousand years ago Jesus was sent by God to this planet to remind us that we were and always have been a child of His. God had never abandoned us. No longer would we need to be preoccupied with our dread of eternal punishment after we finished our earthly sojourns. But the message of Jesus, poorly understood by his disciples and by the religious leaders of his day, and to those following in later centuries, was turned into a new set of rituals, a new set of dogmas. A new religion was created about Jesus instead of the religion of Jesus.

1. *A Course In Miracles, Text*, p. 194.
2. Matthew Fox, *Meditations with Meister Eckart*, p. 15.
3. Pat Rodegast and Judith Stanton, compilers, *Emmanuel's Book*, p. 39.

Chapter 13: The Atonement

Atonement. According to Webster's dictionary the word "atonement" in theological terms means "the redeeming of mankind and the reconciliation of God with man, brought about by Jesus' death." This meaning is accepted by most Christians. Jesus, however, taught differently. The words of Jesus in *A Course in Miracles* do not agree at all with this definition. Jesus explains that the atonement (at-one-ment) means the correction or the undoing of errors. We need to keep in mind that errors are of our minds, not of our bodies, since bodies simply follow the commands of the mind. Even in matters of health, as we saw in Part I in "Creating Reality", only minds get sick, a diseased mind creates the illness of the body. Jesus said that his part in the atonement is the canceling out or undoing of all of our errors. He said that "Spirit is in a state of grace forever. Your reality is only spirit. Therefore you are in a state of grace forever." [1]

The atonement was established at the very moment that the first "tiny mad idea" of separation entered our minds way back before the big bang. It was established "as the means of restoring guiltlessness to minds that have denied it and thus denied Heaven to itself." [2]

Please read that quotation again, for that is the very essence of the atonement. We, in our physical body with the ego directing our thoughts, believe that we are guilty, having forgotten who we really are. We have forgotten, but the Holy Spirit knows that we are sinless and guiltless, The Holy Spirit, then, is busy restoring to our minds (helping us to re-member) the truth about ourselves. In other words, Jesus explained that the atonement is the changing of our mind. Here in our world, our minds are controlled and directed by the fear and guilt of our ego. The Holy Spirit wants us to change our mind, turn a deaf ear to our ego and to remember the Oneness, to change our mind from our little self and to remember our true Self which never left Heaven.

Jesus completed the process of the atonement by completely overcoming the belief in the separation. He completely overcame any fear or guilt and became pure Love. He had only the mind of Christ. As Paul wrote in Philippians 2:5, "Let this mind be in you, which was also in Christ Jesus." And Paul again, in Romans 12:2, said, "Conform not to this world but be ye transformed by the renewing of your mind."

Let's keep reminding ourselves that acceptance of the atonement is only a matter of time. Time was made for just that reason – to allow "time" to overcome the deceit of the ego and to re-member (to restore or put back together) who we are. The ego is simply the belief in the reality of our separated self. Looking back to our discussion of the viewpoint of the physicists and the philosophers, the Self is in the implicate order which is transcendent or outside of our physical reality. Our little self is in the explicate order, the explicated or manifested reality of our three-dimensional world.

In our physical existence, our ego cries out that guilt is real. We all do feel guilty and many Christians that I know love to brag about how sinful and guilty they are, and then, at the same time, many of them in a very smug and elitist fashion proclaim that they have been "saved'. But it is only with the eyes and ears of the ego that we hear and see what we think is reality. We are thoroughly convinced that this physical body of ours, along with all the pain and suffering is "where it is at", but our interpretations of truth are only a result of our belief in the separation. The words of Jesus make this clear:

"You but mistake interpretation for the truth. And you are wrong. But a mistake is not a sin, nor has reality been taken from its throne by your mistakes. God reigns forever, and His laws alone prevail upon you and upon the world. His love remains the only thing there is. Fear Is illusion, for you are like Him." [3]

In short, then, the purpose of the atonement is to restore the awareness of truth. The awareness that we never, in reality, left Home. We never left Heaven. The opposite of love – fear – only exists while we are living in the illusion of our physical nature. The hellfire and brimstone concept became prevalent because of our guilt for having believed in the separation and the belief that punishment must be meted out. That fear is replaced by forgiveness for what we never did (we never did leave the Garden/Paradise/Heaven). But punishment is not called for because in God's sight we are without sin. We are as perfect and as eternal as our Creator, being of his very essence. Jesus said it this way:

"The state of guiltlessness is only the condition in which what is not there has been removed from the disordered mind that thought it was." [4] and "When you feel guilty, remember that the ego has indeed violated the laws of God, but you have not. Leave the 'sins' of the ego to me. That is what Atonement is for." [5]

As Gary Schwartz, our professor of science whom we quoted earlier in Part I, writes: "In fact, according to contemporary field physics, we are never alone – rather we are 'all one'. We need to experience atonement, which is at-one-ment," [6]

When we see the face of Christ – the face of innocence – in

all of our brothers and sisters we will be free from projecting guilt upon ourselves and upon our neighbor. The Atonement will have been accomplished.

1. *A Course in Miracles, Text*, p. 10.
2. *Ibid*, p. 281.
3. *A Course in Miracles, Manual*, p. 47.
4. *A Course in Miracles, Text*, p. 279.
5. *Ibid*, p. 63.
6. Gary E. Schwartz, *The G.O.D. Experiments*, p. 178.

Chapter 14: The Word of God

But one does not eat out of a garden that grew in centuries past."
–Ken Carey

Recently at the morning "celebration" service at the church which I attend most regularly, the pastor made the statement that most Christians use the Bible like a drunk uses a lamppost, for support, instead of for illumination or enlightenment. He said that Christians search the scriptures to "prove" what they already "know" to be their "truth".

I certainly agree with that statement, for in spite of my many doubts and questions, I did some of just that during my early years when I attended the Baptist Church with my family. Until I entered military service I read the Bible regularly, often doing so with an eye to gaining ammunition to confront the "unbelievers".

So, then, let us begin by asking the question: What is the Word of God? Is it the words on the printed page of the Torah and the pages of the New Testament? Are not those texts just words written down by many different persons relating stories handed down by word of mouth many years after the fact? The story of Genesis, in part, recounts the beginning of Creation which took place millions of years before somebody put the story into words. This, of course, was man's way of attempting to explain the unexplainable. For example, the mythological story of Adam and Eve and the subsequent falling into sin, illustrates early man's attempt to understand the story of our apparent separation from our Creator. Yes, I do believe that much of the scriptures were inspired, but much of the original texts have been expurgated, added to and changed, to better conform not only to what the translators held as their truth, but to conform to the expediencies of the time.

The Bible is an anthology of Hebrew and Greek literature, a multitude of different texts and codices gathered together by various councils of Roman Catholic Bishops and declared divinely inspired and canonical three hundred or more years after the life of Jesus. Throughout the following years the early Church debated whether to think of the scriptures as literal truth and as accurate history or to just accept them as allegorical and as a teaching for moral guidance. The Old Testament was often spoken of as "childish". It is mostly the Protestants, especially the fundamentalist branch of Protestantism, that have come to declare that every word of the Bible is the "Word of God", when there are obvious historical contradictions and even when certain passages do not agree with their own "fundamentalist truths." For example, there are two different creation stories in the first two chapters of Genesis and there are three distinct and irreconcilable versions of the Ten Commandments in the Torah. Not to mention that the story of Moses's birth, and being found by the Pharaoh's daughter floating in a basket in the Nile River, was copied from an earlier Sumerian text, *The Epic of Gilgamesh.*

But the priests and ministers of today do more than turn a blind eye to biblical passages that are inconvenient to their "truth." They read and preach their truths from books in the New Testament that are completely bogus writings.

The Second Epistle of Peter is a prime example. "Among modern scholars, there is wide agreement that Second Peter, is a pseudonymous work, that is indeed, many think it is the latest work in the New Testament and assign it to the first or even second quarter of the second century." [1] The Second Epistle of Peter was written 150 years after the death of Peter by an unknown person who fictitiously ascribed his work to Peter. The First Epistle of Peter was dictated by Peter and is considered a true account of Peter's words. Peter, himself, was illiterate, not being able to read or write.

One may be asking at this point, if the Second Epistle of Peter in the New Testament is bogus, why or how did it come to be included in our Bible? It was added to the Canon, the accepted list of books to be included in the Bible in the 4th century at the insistence of Bishop Jerome, against the objections of many other powerful Church leaders. Jerome, sadistic in nature, loved to preach eternal punishment to those who were not believers and devout followers of his Church. The Second Epistle of Peter gave him the authority (excuse) to do so for it clearly indicated eternal punishment by a wrathful God.

Personally, I have always wondered why, after the Protestant Reformation, the various Protestant denominations, that gradually developed because of their differences with Lutheranism, did not want to divorce themselves from the dictates of Romanism. I suspect they, to this day, prefer to put fear into the hearts of their followers – to insure that they still appear on Sundays and fill the church coffers.

John Shelby Spong, an Episcopal bishop for 24 years, an acknowledged lover of the Bible, has some words to say on our subject, "What is the Word of God?"

> "I am a Christian . . . I call Jesus my Lord. I believe that he has mediated God in a powerful and unique way to human history and to me"... BUT, he continues, "I do not believe that the Bible is the word of God, in any literal sense. I do not regard it as the primary source of divine revelation. I do not believe that God dictated it or even inspired it in its entirety. I see the Bible as a human

book mixing the profound wisdom of sages
through the centuries with the limitations of
human perceptions of reality at a particular
time in human history." [2]

Can we not accept the Bible for what it is? Can we not accept that it is a record of how our forebears related to their world? Does it not describe their cosmology, how they made sense of the world about them, and how they related to their God? They could only relate to their world and God with the understanding that they had at that time. Bishop Spong makes it clear: "The Bible becomes not a literal road map to reality but an historic narrative of the journey our religious forebears made in the eternal quest to understand life, the world, themselves, and God." [3]

Today, leaders of all branches of Christianity pick and choose what scriptures to expound upon to better impress their "truths" upon their followers. A few years ago, when visiting my home town in Minnesota, I attended one of the local churches. The young minister preached about sin and the need to be"saved" – the same sermon I had endured so often as a kid. After the service I questioned the pastor about his words and, among other things, I quoted to him the words of Jesus when he said to his disciples, "Ye are gods." The minister's answer was yes, he was aware of that scripture, but it did not conform to the truth as Christianity defined the truth so he ignored it. He pretended, he said, that it wasn't there. Wow! Talk about the blind leading the blind.

But what is the Word of God?"

Perhaps to most of you reading these lines, the Holy Bible is the Word of God. To others it may be the Koran, The Torah, the Book of Mormon or some other holy writing. Whichever writing it is for you, you may believe it is the only true word of God, and you consider other holy books to be less worthy, perhaps even thinking of them as evil. But did you ever stop to think why you accept your particular book as the true word of God? Did you not choose your Holy Scriptures because of the accident of your birth, the country in which you were born, the ethnic background of your family and the religious training given you as a youth?

It is said God spoke to the Israelites through Abraham, Moses and the prophets. To the generations that followed, the words received by the earlier leaders and recorded in the Old Testament became the "Word of God." God had spoken. It was His final Word. His final Law, the last instructions of the Creator to His creation.

Then Jesus came. His followers recorded the story of his life and his teachings as best they could remember and understand them. Thus the New Testament became the Word of God to the Christians. It contained, for them, the final pronouncements from their Creator.

Moslems accept Jesus and his teachings, but believe that the words given to Mohammed are the final Inspired writing to humanity. The Latter Day Saints also accept the New Testament, but claim that the words received by Joseph Smith are the definitive Words of God. Other religions, too, have their "Word of God".

The various holy scriptures that we have mentioned and those of other groups in other parts of the world were transcribed by people believed to be inspired by the Holy Spirit and were meant for those of their day. They were written in the framework of their current understanding of the workings of the cosmos and humanity's place in it.

What about today? Is God no longer interested in us and what happens to us on this planet? Is God no longer communicating with us? Has He forsaken us? I do not believe that He has.

It seems to me that God is now speaking, as never before, through the Holy spirit, to the peoples of this world, bringing the teachings of love to a higher octave of understanding. Today we have a much more enlightened understanding of our place and purpose in the cosmos and are ready to receive divine truths of a higher order.

I believe that the Holy Spirit is speaking to people all over the world – to the Jew, the Hindu, the Christian, the Moslem and those of all faiths, as well as to those of no faith. To many, His truths are heard in subtle ways, the receiver never guessing from where

(X) Kenneth Wapnick, at the age of 71, left this world in January, 2014.

his ideas, thoughts and revelations are coming. God is whispering to us through the trees, the wind, the mountains. God is speaking to us through the words of a stranger, the look of a child, a photo in a newspaper. What do we hear when we sit quietly by a gently flowing stream and dream or meditate? What inspiration of peace and harmony do we feel when we gaze upon the distant mountains and watch at sunset as the colors imperceptibly change from pink to crimson to dark blue and purple?

To many others the Holy Spirit is speaking more directly through the process commonly called "channeling". There are a great number of incredibly beautiful and inspired writings transcribed by God-loving souls from directions given them by those in the spirit world. These inspired (in-the-Spirit) channeled writings themselves tell us that this phenomenon will increase for a period, but become unnecessary when very soon each of us will be receptive directly to the prompting and teaching of the Holy Spirit.

Again we ask: What is the "Word of God?"

We have been speaking of the various holy books – inspired writings of different peoples and their religious beliefs, their "truths". But these writings are just words on paper. The words themselves are just a means of transmitting information. Words are just symbols of reality just as physical objects in our world are illusory, just symbols of the real world in the "implicate order" of the physicist. Just as Plato called our three - dimensional reality a pale shadow of the real world. *Conversations with God* says it this way: "Words are merely utterances: noises that stand for feelings, thoughts and experience. They are Symbols, Signs, Insignia. They are not Truth. They are not the real thing." [4]

One last time: What is the "Word of God"?

"In the beginning was the Word, the Word was with God and Word was God...and the Word became flesh and dwelt among us." This passage in the Gospel of John shows us that the "Word of God" existed from the beginning and now the Word had become flesh as Jesus, the Son of God. God's Son is the word of God. And who is God's Son? You are. You are the Word of God.

1. *New American Bible, Introduction to the Second Epistle of Peter.*
2. John Shelby Spong, *A New Christianity For a New World*, pp. 6-7.
3. *Ibid*, p. 33.
4. Neale Donald Walsch, *Conversations With God, Book I*, p. 4.

Chapter 15: The Lord's Prayer

It has become part of the liturgy or ritual for Christian churches to repeat in word or in song, the Lord's Prayer. Even in the little Baptist Church which I attended with my family in a small community in Minnesota, a church which ridiculed the rituals of the Lutheran Church and believed the liturgies and rituals of the Roman Catholic Church to be inspired by Satan, repeated the Lord's Prayer.

As a child, later as a young man, and even into adulthood I was confused with the phrase: "Lead us not into temptation". Everybody, like sheep, without thought mouthed the phrase. Did no one question or wonder as I did what it really meant? I never could accept the idea that we, as children of God, needed to ask God to not tempt us to do wrong. The words of Jesus will help in understanding the phrase: "Let us not let littleness lead God's Son (each one of us) into temptation. His (God's son) is beyond it, measureless and timeless as eternity." [1]

God is not in the business of tempting His children, who are a part of Him. God knows who we are. God knows of our perfection. God knows that we are One with Him, only having lost – temporarily – our awareness of that fact.

The phrase ending the Lord's Prayer as it appears in the King

James version of the Bible does not exist in the original manuscripts. The words, "For thine is the Kingdom, the Power and the Glory forever, Amen." were added in medieval times by an overly enthusiastic monk because he felt that it gave a beautiful flourish to the text. (And it does!) Even to write of this historic fact is anathema to the fundamentalists. They do not wish to be confused by the facts or to know truth, only to believe blindly in every literal word in what they perceive to be the "Word of God".

A Course in Miracles gives this prayer by Jesus. I believe that these are the words of Jesus when he gave what has become to be known as the Lord's Prayer:

Forgive us our illusions, Father, and help us to accept our true relationship with You, in which there are no illusions, and where none can ever enter. Our holiness is yours. What can there be in us that needs forgiveness when Yours is perfect? The sleep of forgetfulness is only the unwillingness to remember Your forgiveness and Your Love. Let us not wander into temptation, for the temptation of the Son of God is not Your Will. And let us receive only what You have given, and accept but this into the minds which You created and which You love. Amen." [2]

1. *A Course in Miracles, Text*, p. 486.
2. *Ibid*, p. 350.

Chapter 16: Evil

"What seem to be evils are not actually such."
–Seneca B.C. 4 - A.D. 66

In the eternal scheme of things, is there such a thing as evil? Let us take a look at that question.

The source of light on our earth is the sun. There is no source for darkness. Darkness is simply the absence of light. One can dispel darkness with a flashlight. One cannot dispel light with a flashdark! Similarly, the source of heat is also the sun. Coldness is the absence of heat, there being no source of coldness.

Let us look at evil in the same way. The source of all goodness is God. There is no source for evil, evil being the absence of goodness. Some may answer that the source of evil is the devil, but then what is the source of the devil (assuming for the moment that there is an entity called the devil)? It must be God. Would God create evil?

Everything in our world is based on polarities: hot-cold, up-down, beautiful-ugly, peace- war. love-fear, goodness-evil, etc. Could we know what hot was unless we had experienced cold? Or peace without conflict? If there were no darkness, would there even be a word for light? If there were only goodness, we wouldn't know what the word goodness meant. Only in this three-dimensional universe do we experience these polarities. So it seems that the apparent existence of evil on earth is part of the illusion of living inside of time and space. In God's reality, where there are no spatial or temporal qualities, there is only pure love. Where there is only pure love, fear seems to be an illusion. As Jesus said, "the opposite of love is fear, but what is all encompassing can have no opposite." [1] And recall, too, the words of St.. Paul when he said that "perfect love casteth out fear."

There have been wise men who have understood this in centuries past. Epicetus, one of the stoic writers of the early Roman Empire, put it this way: "When a man speaks evil or does evil to you, remember that he does or says it because he thinks it is fitting for him. It is not possible for him to follow what seems good to you, but only what seems good to him."

After what has been said here about evil being only illusory, there may be a deeper reality that better explains the concept of evil. According to the cutting edge physics of David Bohm, all polarities or opposites are not really opposites at all. What we see as negatives and opposites really represent deep unities that man cannot truly comprehend. In this sense, evil and goodness are necessary parts of a whole. Eastern philosophical thought teaches the same concept, that truth is grasped through the synthesis of apparent opposites and that humanity's distorted perceptions cause incorrect assumptions. Seth agrees: "Opposites have validity only in your own system of reality. They are a part of your root assumptions, and so you must deal with them as such. They represent, however, deep unities that you do not understand." [2]

These ideas of evil which we have explored are summed up beautifully in the words of Emmanuel: [3]

> "Evil is only ignorance of Divine Will and
> Divine Law. None would resist Divine Law
> if they were aware that it consists of their
> own bliss and eternal happiness. Although the
> negative energies may seem not to flow with

God's natural laws, they are indeed present in your physical world doing God's work. Without them you would not be offered a choice between darkness and Light and your growth process would be much hindered. So, you see, they are a necessary ingredient. These energies are not masters, they are servants of God's Will."

1. *A Course in Miracles*, Introduction.
2. Jane Roberts, *Seth Speaks: The Eternal Validity of the soul*, p. 406.
3. *Emmanuel's Book*, compiled by Pat Rodegast and Judith Stanton, p. 85.

Chapter 17: What is Sin?

*"Be willing, then, to see your brother sinless, that
Christ may rise before your vision and give you
joy."*
—A Course In Miracles

Is there any subject dearer to the heart of fundamentalist Christians than the subject of sin and salvation? "Have you been saved? Are you born again?" Are these not the questions that a Christian directs to the stranger, to the visitor of his place of worship, to his fellow worker? Having myself been brought up in a fundamentalist Baptist home, I am well accustomed to such questions.

All of mankind, each and every one of us, I feel, must admit to ourselves that we are not always perfect in our actions and certainly not without malice in our thoughts toward one another (we are not always thinking loving thoughts). Yes, it seems to me, we have all "sinned" in both thought and action. Yes, we have all "sinned" against each other. And yes, some have even cursed their Creator. But are these wrong thoughts and actions sin? Consider this for a moment: maybe we are not sinners.

Of course, it depends on how one defines sin. Before considering the literal meaning of the word, which is also the meaning given to it by St. Paul, let us look at the concept of sin as usually taught by both Protestant and Catholic Christians. Sin is a concept generally defined by Christians as any action, word or thought that separates them from God. In short, sin is anything that requires forgiveness and atonement.

If sin, as we have so far defined it, is what separated us from our God, perhaps we should question once again, as we have in other chapters of this book, whether it is even possible to become separated from God. Did we become separated from the One who created us before the beginning of time? Did we become separated when we first had that "tiny mad idea" of separation? Were we separated from God at our physical birth because of the sin of Adam? Is it possible to become separated from God because of our individual short-comings? In short, are we sinners? Is it possible that we could really be separated from our Creator?

Now, let's look at sin in the more literal and Biblical sense as defined by St. Paul. The word "sin" literally means "missing the mark". This is the generally understood meaning imparted to the word by the Gospels and by St. Paul in his epistles. Sin is a failure on our part to be completely centered in God. Sin is to be imperfect in our words, actions and thoughts. As explained so beautifully and logically in *A Course in Miracles*, we humans condemn ourselves by our sinning, by missing the mark "of the high calling of God in Jesus Christ." God does not condemn us, we do not need to ask Him for forgiveness, for He forgave us before we were born. He forgave us not for any sin we have committed (for it is impossible to sin in the sense of causing a separation), but He forgives us for forgetting who we are, for forgetting our divinity and for believing that we can successfully hide from Him in our ego bodies. Recall that we, in our guilt, created our perception of the universe as a place to hide from God.

We, however, must forgive the world and everybody in it for all the wrongs which we have imagined have been done to us. *A Course In Miracles* says it this way:

"When the thought of separation has been changed to one of true forgiveness, will the world be seen in quite another light; and one which leads to truth, where all its errors vanish." [1]

The core teaching of Jesus was to "repent and believe the Gospel." (Matthew 4:17) The Greek word translated as "repent" in our Bible, is metanoia, which literally means "going beyond, or higher, than the mind." St. Paul defined it as the renewing of our mind in Christ. Metanoia is the state of consciousness where we transcend the ego with all of the hate, fear and selfishness that separate us from the true awareness of our divinity. Jesus said that we should love our enemies. When we learn to truly love all of creation, then we are beginning to transcend our ego.

Note that the ego and the human state of consciousness does not separate us from God, for that would not be possible, but it separates us from knowing that we are one with God. True repentance brings the awareness that the kingdom of God is within. The disciples one day asked Jesus where heaven was. Jesus answered by saying not to look up into the "heavens" for heaven. The kingdom of heaven, he said, was within them. In other words, heaven is the soul, the real me, the real you. So why do the preachers still talk about going to heaven when our bodies die? Do they not read the scriptures? We are the kingdom of heaven! In *A Course In Miracles*, Jesus says that if we ask where heaven or anything is, we just do not understand. There is no where: all is One. Also recall that Jesus said," you are one with me as I am one with the Father" and in John 10:34 he reminded the disciples of their divinity by saying, "Is it not written in your law, I said Ye are gods?".

In the most recent translation of the letters of Paul, the original King James reading of Romans 3:9 has been changed from "they are all under sin" to read, "a disregard of the law". Paul then says "in universal terms, there is no such thing as sin ... the teaching of sin is a means of coercion through fear," [2] Jesus, overlighted by the Christ, demonstrated to us by his life, death and resurrection that all of God's creation will become perfected as he was, but it is each person's decision as to when that will happen.

Matthew Fox, in his book, Original Blessing, demonstrates that the Fall/Redemption model of spirituality is not in the Bible and was not mentioned by any Christian writer before the life and writings of St. Augustine, a Roman Catholic monk of medieval times who wrestled mightily with his own terrible pangs of guilt. Fox uses the term "creation spirituality" for what the scriptures teach in place of the Fall/Redemptions model of St. Augustine and subsequent theology.

The thesis of Fox, taken from the Old Testament, is that humanity was born with original blessing, not original sin. The Old Testament does not teach original sin. The Old Testament is the sacred book of the Jewish people. If original sin were taught in it, the Jewish rabbis would certainly be aware of it. The great teacher, Rabbi Elie Wiesel, agrees, for he wrote in his book, *Messengers of God*, that the idea of original sin was alien to Jewish tradition.

In *A Course in Miracles*, Jesus is quoted as saying that when you are tempted to believe in sin, you should remember this:

> "If sin is real, both God and you are not. If creation is extension, the Creator must have extended Himself, and it is impossible that what is part of Him is totally unlike the rest. If sin is real, God must be at war with Himself. He must be split, and torn between good and evil, partially sane and partially insane. For He must have created what wills to destroy Him and has the power to do so. Is it not easier to believe that you have been mistaken than to believe in this?" [3]

According to the Bible, God is not willing that one soul be lost. Can one countermand God's will? Eventually each and every one

of God's sons and daughters will be healed of the imagined separation and return to the awareness of who he or she is. Everyone is
on a path to this awareness, back to God. Some, it seems from our
human viewpoint, are on a more direct path than others, but none
can be lost in the eternal sense. We are lost only in the sense that
we have wandered off our path, taken all sorts of detours and gotten
stuck for a time in the mire of the world's temptations and allure-
ments. Many of us, too, have gotten lost in religion, in rituals and
ceremonies, repeating endless prayers, believing that somebody or
something outside of ourselves is necessary to save us from punishment or even annihilation. When we first accepted the idea of
separation, guilt entered and the ego took basic control. When we
accept the atonement, the idea of separation will be ended. Guilt is
what hides the face of Christ from us. God's Son – each one of us
– is blameless, guiltless and sinless. The atonement (at-one-ment)
is mankind's final lesson,

> "For it teaches him that, never having sinned,
> he has no need of salvation. . . That is why
> atonement centers on the past, which is the
> source of separation, and where it must be
> undone. For separation must be corrected
> where it was made." [4]

Salvation, then, which eventually will come to every soul,
however long it may seem to take, is achieved when we recognize
the guiltlessness of the Son of God, each one of us recognizing our
innocence. God created us. He knows what (who) we are. He knows
that He created us out of Himself and that we remain within Him.
He knows, as we will come to know, our guiltlessness. No one is
without His holiness. No one unworthy of His love.

The crucifixion showed that one can assault the body and even
destroy it. But anything that can be assaulted or destroyed is not real
(because the real world is as eternal as God Himself). The crucifixion taught us that we (the real Self, the soul) cannot be assaulted

or destroyed, and through the resurrection we know that the Spirit, the soul, is eternal.

A favorite verse for Christian fundamentalism is John 3:3 where Jesus said "Ye must be born again," Jesus has clarified this by saying "I am the model for rebirth, but rebirth is merely the dawning on your mind of what is already in it. God placed it there Himself, and so it is true forever." [5]

Another favorite verse of Christian fundamentalism, especially of the televangelists, and which was the center of innumerable sermons that I suffered through as a Baptist youth, is Romans 6:23: "For the wages of sin is death; but the gift of God is eternal life through Jesus our Lord."

The fundamentalist Christian would say that verse means that if he commits sin he is condemned to a hell of eternal punishment by a wrathful God, but, if he is born again, accepting Jesus as his personal savior, he will gain eternal life. Wow! Is there anything in those words about a hell or a devil? Does it say anything about being condemned by a wrathful God? Do even the words "saved" or "born again" appear in that passage? Obviously the answer is "no". Then, maybe we should stop and ask ourselves where those imaginative ideas come from.

I have attempted to show in Part I of this book, and again in many chapters of Part II, that the world we perceive is the illusory world of separation from God. The physical world was "made" (perceived) by us, not by the Creator of All That Is. "God so loved the world that he gave his only begotten son," (John 3:16.) God does love the real world, heaven, but does not perceive our physical world which is the symbol of death and is only an illusion,. God has knowledge. He does not perceive. In the real world, heaven, all is eternal, there is no death. In our temporary illusionary world our body does die as a consequence of the "sins" of the flesh, but we, as souls, are eternal, without beginning and without ending, as eternal and guiltless as our Creator of which we are part.

1. *A Course in Miracles*, Workbook for students, p. 413.
2. Hilarion, *The Letters of Paul*, p. 31.
3. *A Course in Miracles, Text*, p. 465.
4. *Ibid*, pp., 237, 356.
5. *Ibid*, p. 94.

To Hell With Hell

Chapter 18: Forgiveness

"Forgiveness ... is still, and quietly does nothing.
It offends no aspect of reality, nor seeks to twist it
to appearances it likes. It merely looks and waits,
and judges not."
–A Course in Miracles

It is easy to say, " I forgive you," but it is difficult for us to truly forgive. Often we say that we forgive someone without really meaning it. We say, "I forgive you," to our child, to our spouse or to a friend. Perhaps it is after a mild family disagreement or after some more serious difference with a friend or co-worker. But do we always mean it when we say it? Do we sometimes inwardly say, "Yes, I forgive you this time, but I'll always remember what you did and you'd better not do it again?" Is that truly forgiving?

If we truly forgive someone for what they did or said to or about us, we would really forget the incident, restoring our relationship to what it was before the incident. True forgiveness (fore-giveness) implies that it is as though the incident never happened ..

But, why in the first place, do we find it necessary to forgive? The need for forgiveness implies that we perceive that someone has attacked us. If we forgive someone for attacking us, it means that we have seen sin or wrongdoing in the attacker. We are saying to him, in effect, that even thought he has done something wrong, we will forgive him and perhaps pray for his sinful soul. Are we not thus establishing the sin and then forgiving it. That is a contradiction.

When we forgive wrongdoing in others or when we acknowledge wrongdoing in our own life, we are identifying others and ourselves with the body. Only a body can suffer and commit error. The real Self, the soul, the divine part of us, cannot suffer or commit error.

TWO STEPS IN FORGIVENESS

First of all, it is important to remember that forgiveness has nothing to do with God forgiving us. He knows who we are – his perfect, eternal Son in whom He is well pleased.

Secondly, we must learn to forgive ourselves. We forgive ourselves for believing that we became separated from our Father, Creator of All That Is. We forgive ourselves for believing that God is a vengeful God who will judge us at some future judgment day and find us guilty. We forgive ourselves for believing that we are sinners and need to be "saved" to escape from an eternity of separation from our Creator.

But, you say, it is not easy to forgive ourselves. True, so we begin by first forgiving others. We forgive them for what we imagine them having done to us. Recall, the admonition of Jesus in Matthew 7, "Judge not that you be not judged" and not to complain about the moat in our brother's eye until we have removed the beam from our own eye.

It may be helpful when practicing forgiveness of others to keep in mind that each person is at a different stage in his or her soul development and that each person is doing the very best he or she knows how with his or her present understanding. We forgive this person while not condoning the deed he or she may have committed. A murderer must be separated from society, but we can completely forgive him or her, knowing that we are forgiving ourselves for the murderous thoughts we have had. We recognize in the murderer our bother or sister in Christ for we are One.

Our relationship with others is our practice field. The more difficult the relationship, the greater the opportunity for learning forgiveness. We should be thankful for out friends, for our fellow workers, for the boss or whoever it might be who creates the most difficult situations and problems in our life. It is through the process of forgiveness in such situations that our greatest learning takes place.

Jesus suggested that when we look upon a brother or sister we should say to ourselves, " I thank you, Father, for your perfect Son and in his glory I will see my own." [1]

1. *A Course In Miracles, Text*, p. 640.

Chapter 19: Judgment

*"Only humans are judgmental, and because you
are, you assume that I must be. Yet I am not – and
that is a great truth you cannot accept."*
–*Conversations With God*

We are standing in the checkout line in the supermarket. Today, instead of browsing the gossip in the tabloids to pass the time, we become a people watcher. In our minds we begin to criticize each person waiting in line ahead of us. We criticize their looks, their clothes and their actions.

It is easy, isn't it, to judge and to criticize everyone around us, our wife or husband, our boss, our subordinates, our neighbors and even the President of the United States? But could we not practice a little tolerance and practice accepting others as they are? When in line at the checkout counter we can look at each person with love even while we recognize their physical imperfections. We can look beyond the physical and remember that within each body there is a soul, a child of God. We can be aware that each person we come into contact with, and even those we read about, are doing the best they know how with the understanding they have. Each of us is at a different point in our soul's journey. The one we criticize may act negatively in things they little understand whereas others may know truths that we have not yet learned.

The biblical teaching in Matthew 7 says that if we do not judge others we will not be judged. We attract to ourselves the same energy that we send to others. If we accept our brother with understanding and compassion, we will receive the same understanding and compassion from him.

But how we love to judge others! Why do we not see the log in our eye before we criticize the small splinter in our brother's eye?

And we also love to judge ourselves. How the Fundamentalist loves to beat his chest, proudly exulting that he is a sinner, often bragging that he is or was a bigger sinner than others. How the Christians flock to hear the visiting evangelist from a distant city who is billed as a former gangster! The worse his sin has been, the more the crowd wants to hear him. We love to call ourselves sinners and display our guilt. Loudly proclaiming our sin and guilt somehow seems to lessen the pain. As Emmanuel says in the following passage, if we learn to accept ourselves and others, there will be no need for forgiveness and no need to feel guilty.

> "How can you not forgive yourself for being exactly who you are? To find the God within you, you must go through the portal of self-acceptance as you are now. Yes, all your faults and imperfections, all your little secrets, fearful uglinesses that you are loathe to admit to yourself, are already known. They are part of your Divine Plan. True acceptance bypasses the need for self-forgiveness. [1]

The writer of Matthew 7 is not in any way saying that if we judge others God will judge us. God does not judge. He sees us clearly for what we are – His Sons and Daughters, who are as pure, perfect and eternal as Himself. Jesus achieved Christhood when he became fully conscious that he was a Son of God, and told his disciples that they were too ("You are one with me as I am one with the Father"), that God would not judge them and that they should not judge one another.

When we can see ourselves as children of God, knowing that we – our real self, the Christ within – are perfect, sinless creatures, we cannot but accept ourselves and love ourselves without reservation. Then our love will embrace the whole world and the whole world will embrace us! Our entire being will shine with the love and joy of our Creator. Our love and joy will be apparent to everyone. No longer will we blame someone or something for anything in our lives, because, if we do, we realize that we are really blaming ourselves. Worse, we are blaming God.

It has been for me, and I believe for most of my readers, very difficult to accept the fact that we are all without sin and that we are guiltless. When we look at ourselves, our actions, our thoughts, and when we look at the actions of those about us, we certainly feel that we all must be guilty. We judge ourselves guilty. We judge those about us guilty. Yes, while we are living on this planet and clothed in our physical bodies, we are forgetful of who we are and live under the control of our egos. The book, *Conversations with God*, explains it this way:

> "You have projected the role of 'parent' onto God, and thus have come up with a God who judges and rewards or punishes, based on how good he feels about what you've been up to. But this is a simplistic view of God, based on your mythology." [2]

Why did the mob condemn Jesus to death? Was it not because he claimed that the Son of God was guiltless? The mob in Jerusalem became furious, believing that Jesus's claim of innocence was blasphemy. We, following the desire of our egos, are still demanding crucifixion of ourselves, demanding that we pay the price for our guilt. All we need do is to accept the truth of who we are. Should we not take God at his word? Let us not call God a liar. Let us not deny the words of Jesus. God's Son is guiltless.

THE LAST JUDGMENT

The Last Judgment! What a frightening prospect! We picture ourselves standing on the "last day" before God, who sits on His throne with Jesus standing at His right side. God looks directly into our eyes and is about ready to make His last judgment of us. He will either say, "Depart from me into utter darkness. I never knew you. You are condemned to suffer everlasting punishment in a hell that I have prepared for you." Or He will pass us through the pearly gates into the kingdom of heaven where we will walk on streets paved with gold and be given a harp to play and sing His praises for eternity.

Is not the above a fair description of the average Christian's image of the Last Judgment? Let us examine some of the details of that picture. First, it is very anthropomorphic, is it not? We have a God in the form of a man, sitting on a throne with Jesus, who appears in his earthly physical form at God's right side. Then we have the gates of pearl and the streets of gold. It seems we are to continue to enjoy our material riches.

Where is Heaven? Did not Jesus say in response to a disciple's question that the kingdom of heaven was in them – that we (our souls) are the kingdom of heaven?

And what about hell in our picture of the Last Judgement ? If heaven is up there somewhere, then hell must be down below somewhere. But God must be there, too, if he is present everywhere. And is God not pure love? Could love prepare a hell with everlasting punishment?

Obviously, the Last Judgment is badly misinterpreted and misunderstood by the average religious person. As described above, the Last Judgment has been and is still used by Fundamentalist preachers to scare their listeners into accepting their brand of religion. But nothing could be further from the truth. "Their is no judgment in what you call the afterlife. You will not even be allowed to judge yourself (for you would surely give yourself a low score, given how judgmental and unforgiving you are with yourself in this life)". [3]

Let's go back to that dramatic scene where we are standing before God awaiting His judgment. Is it even conceivable that our Creator would not recognize his Creation, His own Son? Can God judge humanity, a creation of His, part of His own being? Is it conceivable that God could separate part of Himself from Himself? Is it not insanity to think so? Is it not arrogant to call God a liar for proclaiming His son guiltless? Apparently we think we know better, and proclaim ourselves sinners and worthy of eternal punishment.

There never has been any judgment on the part of God. Only after the imagined Separation, when after eons of time we fled from the mythological Garden of Eden, has there been the concept of judgment, the idea of choosing between what is good and what is evil. The only judging that has been done and is being done is by ourselves, of ourselves. The "final judgment" of ourselves by ourselves will not entail any punishment. On the contrary, it will heal our sense of separation from God and release us from all of our guilt and pain.

It seems that judgment is a continuing process we go through during our lives on earth until we realize that we do not need to seek salvation through priests, rituals or adherence to any set of rules or dogmas, whether of a fundamentalist or other religious persuasion. The case that man has built against himself would have to be dismissed by the highest ultimate court because there can be no case against a Son or Daughter of God, for that is tantamount to a case against God.

The Last Judgment for each of us will be the moment when we know fully that God has already judged us perfect. It will happen when we finally realize that we do not need God's forgiveness and when we can accept ourselves as perfect, sinless creatures. The Last Judgment for each of us will be when we finally hear the words of God welcoming us home – home with Him whom we never left! Jesus says it this way:

This is God's final Judgment: You are still My Holy Son forever innocent, forever loving and forever loved, as limitless, as your Creator, and completely changeless and forever pure. Therefore, awaken and return to me. I am Your Father and you are My Son." [4]

1. *Emmanuel's Book*, p. 102.
2. Neale Donald Walsch, *Conversations With God, Book I*, p. 19.
3. *Ibid*, p. 183.
4. *A Course In Miracles, Workbook*, p. 455.

Chapter 20: Sexuality

*In the moment of your creation, you were given
incredible gifts; and one of the most important is
the gift of sexuality!*
    –Bartholomew

(This essay was taken from the author's earlier book, *We Are
One – A Challenge To Traditional Christianity*, written in 1995. It
was very much ahead of it's time, when written, and very appropri-
ate now.)

I can well imagine that many casual readers (especially bookstore browsers) have turned to this essay first - irresistibly drawn
to it by the hint of something forbidden or erotic. Why are we so
titillated by the subject of sex?

There are those who find every reference to sex, or even any
slightly revealing photograph, obscene or dirty, something to avoid.
Often, however, those same persons go out of their way looking
for the obscene so they can register their objection to it. Such as
the man who wrote a letter to the editor of one of the major daily
newspapers in which he indicated that he had taken great offense to
a picture of a little girl published earlier in that paper. He claimed

that the photograph had revealed a small part of the girl's genital area. He discovered that fact, he said, by scrutinizing the photo with a magnifying glass!

There are those who greatly enjoy telling off-color, sexually oriented jokes. These are often the same persons who verbally or sexually abuse others and/or the ones who brazenly leer or make obscene gestures to impress their peers.

Why are we in the Western world, especially those of us in the United States, so obsessed with sex?

The Christian believes, along with those of other faiths, that God made humans male and female, endowing them with sexual organs. Therefore He certainly intended that male and female come together physically and be as one. The fact that we are sexual beings is perfectly natural and normal. Why, then, do we snicker when we hear about a friend's sexual improprieties? Why; then, do we enjoy the lurid stories of the sexual lives of the rich and famous? Why are we so embarrassed about sex that we cannot teach our children about it? Why are so many of us afraid of sex education in our schools?

Is it guilt? Many, perhaps most of us, feel guilty about having sexual feelings. We feel even more guilty and sinful when we give in to those feelings. Why is there rape, incest and sexual abuse of children? I believe it is because we are overridden with guilt due to our Judeo-Christian heritage. Our whole 'society is immersed in the taboos of the Old Testament, those taboos of the Hebrews written to ensure for them a large progeny for military fodder - for their security and victory over their enemies during their wandering in the wilderness. I believe that the unconscious mind of Western culture has been seared with guilt about its sexuality. The rest of the world experiences this guilt also, but perhaps less so.

Guilt has caused many people to repress their sexual instincts in the attempt to conform to the laws and mores of their parents, their church and society in general. Some people, when they no longer can suppress their feelings or conform to the dictates of society, commit rape, child abuse, incest etc. Or, as in the case of teenage homosexuals, they commit suicide. What would happen if all laws regulating sex were abolished?

Bartholomew, channeled by Mary Margaret Moore, suggests just that. Most readers, I imagine, would express horror at such a development, believing that man would become uncontrolled in his passions and "become some kind of sexual beast"[1] as Bartholomew says it. But he argues, and I agree, that the opposite would happen: that an awareness within us would regulate our sexuality much better than any law ever has or ever could. Seth enthusiastically agrees when he says, "Many of you are afraid that without a feeling of guilt there would be no inner discipline, and the world would run wild. It is running quite wild now not despite your ideas of guilt and punishment, but largely because of them."[2]

So it seems that all the laws throughout the world have not deterred man from seeking sexual satisfaction, whether it be legal in his particular society or not.

As an example, let us consider the subject of homosexuality. Homosexuality has been considered an abomination by the Judeo-Christian world. In most other societies it has been understood somewhat better and accepted more freely. Hopefully, with new scientific evidence linking the inclination toward same-sex relationships with genetics, people will learn to be more tolerant. But why the intolerance in the first place? It is generally agreed that approximately one-sixth of the world's population is homosexual or strongly bisexual.[3] This is as true today as it has been in all past historical periods and all societies or cultures of which we have knowledge.

What is perversion? Is it not perversion when one goes contrary to his or her own nature? If it is one's nature to find sexual satisfaction in the opposite sex, then it would be an act of perversion to have a sexual relationship with a member of your own sex. If it is one's nature to find true love and satisfaction only from one's own sex, then it would be a perversion to have a sexual relationship with a member of the opposite sex. Jason suggests that each person should make his own choice and not let society impose a particular expression of sexuality. He says, "Be free, then, to make choices of male and female, male and male, or female and female according to what is truly your preference . . ."[4]

Bartholomew says much the same when he declares that each of us must do what makes us feel creative, loving and positive, because if we attempt to follow the codes of our society against our nature, we will become confused and conflicted in our emotional and spiritual life, ending up angry, resentful and judgmental. He adds, "You believe that God cares in the most minute detail what you do with your sexuality. But He doesn't care. That is your business . . . He has only one concern, and that is the quality of your awareness, your power, your love, and your compassion."[5]

Today's fundamentalist Christians, especially those who follow Pat Robertson, Jerry Falwell and others of the extreme political right wing, single out for their denunciation anything that seems to them to be sins of the flesh. For example, they love to condemn homosexuals to the "fires of hell." They excuse their contempt and hatred of the homosexual by their interpretation of certain passages, especially those from the Book of Leviticus. They seem to be adept at overlooking other passages of the Old Testament (many of which are also in Leviticus) that equally prohibit and condemn sexual acts the heterosexual is more likely to commit. One who commits adultery is condemned, and one who commits onanism is sentenced to *death*. It is hard to believe that was the punishment for simply spilling one's seed upon the ground. I would guess that every man is guilty of that one!

Those religious leaders who self-righteously condemn those who have loving relationships different from those they themselves have are just continuing the age-old conspiracy against individual freedom. Since almost the beginning of man's sojourn on this planet there has been a conspiracy of distortion and lies to make man feel guilty about his sexuality. Both political and religious leaders have fostered the idea of human guilt and continue to try to expand their control thereby. Barbara Marciniak's source, in her channeled book *Bringers of the Dawn*, says[6]:

> The orgasm has been distorted from its
> original purpose. Your body has forgotten
> the cosmic orgasm of which it is capable
> because society has taught you for thousands
> and thousands of years that sexuality is bad.
> You have been taught this in order for you
> to be controlled and to keep you from seek-
> ing the freedom available through sexuality.
> Sexuality connects you with a frequency of
> ecstasy, which connects you back to your
> divine source and to information.

Sexuality was given to mankind as a great gift from God. Through the sexual experience we can discover our true being, we can discover who we are. In our sexual experience we become one with another human, but we are in actuality seeking unity with God. If we did not have all of that guilt in our sexual relationships we would more truly experience, in the coming together with the one we love, the oneness of all; we would become aware of the fact that we truly are a son or daughter of the Creator and that we are indeed one with God.

I do not believe that God judges us on the level of our sexuality. God is only interested in the level of our love, in the level of our understanding. In God there is neither male nor female. There is only one God, of which everyone of us is a part.

I believe that in the remaining few years of this century we will clear out the negativities of our understanding of our sexuality and understand that the sexual coming together of two in an act of love is one sure way of connecting to our higher self and to our Creator.

1. Bartholomew, *I Come as a Brother*. High Mesa Press, Taos, New Mexico, 1986, p. 23.

2. Jane Roberts, *The Nature of Personal Reality*. Prentice Hall, Englewood Cliffs, New Jersey, 1974, p. 68.

3. Jess Stearn, *The Sixth Man*. Doubleday &: Co., New York, 1961.

4. Ron Goettsche and Bob Fogg, Down to Earth. Synergy Publishers, Denver, Colorado, 1984, p. 52.

5. Bartholomew, *op. cit.*, p. 22.

6. Barbara Marciniak, *Bringers of the Dawn*. Bear & Co., Santa Fe, New Mexico, 1992, p. 211.

Bibliography

A Course in Miracles, Foundation for Inner Peace, Huntington Station, N. Y., 1975.

Braden, Gregg, *Fractal Time*, Hay House, Carlsbad, Ca., 2009.

_____, *Deep Truth*, Hay House, Carlsbad, Ca., 2011.

_____, *The Divine Matrix*, Hay House, Carlsbad, Ca., 2007.

Clow, Barbara Hand, *The Pleidian Agenda*, Bear & Co.,Santa Fe, New Mexico, 1995.

Cranston, S. and C. Williams, editors, Reincarnation, *A New Horizon in Science, Religion and Society*, Julian Press, New York, N.Y., 1984.

Crockett, William, *Four Views on Hell*, Grand Rapids: Zondervan, 1992.

Essene, Virginia, *New Teachings for an Awakening Humanity*, S.E.E. Publishing Co., Santa Clara, California, 1986.

Ferverda, Julie, *Raising Hell*, Vagabond Group, Sandpoint, Id., 2014.

Fox, Matthew, *The Coming of the Cosmic Christ*, Harper & Row, New York, N.Y., 1988.

Friedman, Norman, *Bridging Science and Spirit*, Living Books, St. Louis, Missouri, 1994.

Goswami, Amit, *The Self-Aware Universe*, Tarcher/Putnam, New York, N. Y., 1993.

Gregg, Steve, *All You Wanted to Know About Hell*, Harper Collins Christian Publishing Co., 2013.

Hawking, Stephen W., *A Brief History of Time*, Bantam, New York, N. Y.,19

Head, J. and S. L. Cranston, *Reincarnation in World Thought*, Julian Press, New York, N. Y., 1967.

_____, *Reincarnation : The Phoenix Fire Mystery*, Julian Press, New York, N.Y., 1967.

Hilarion, *The Letters of Paul*, Triad, Ashland, Oregon, 1989.

Icke, David, *Remember Who We Are*, David Icke Books, Ltd, Isle of Wight, 2012.

Jampolsky, Gerald G., *Love is Letting Go of Fear*, Celestial Arts, Berkeley, California, 1988.

Jenkins, John Major, *Maya Cosmogenesis 2012*, Bear & Co., 1998.

Lea, Henry Charles, *The Inquisition of the Middle Ages*, Macmillan, New York, 1961.

Lehman, Cale, *The Book of Andrew*, The Round House Press, Kent, Connecticut, 2013.

Marciniak, Barbara, *Bringers of the Dawn*, Bear & Co., Santa Fe, New Mexico, 1992.

Mitchell, Steven, *The Gospel According to Jesus*, Harper Collins, New York, 1991.

Pagels, Elaine, *The Gnostic Gospels*, Random House, New York, 1979.

Popul Vuh, Translated by Dennis Tedlock, Touchstone, Simon & Schuster, New York, 1985.

Primack, Joel and Abrams, Nancy Ellen, *The View From the Center of the Universe*, Penguin Books, New York, 2006.

Purcell, Boyd C., *Spiritual Terrorism*, Author House, 1663 Liberty Drive, Bloomington, In., 2008.

Puryear, Herbert Bruce, *Why Jesus Taught Reincarnation*, New Paradigm Press, Scottsdale, Arizona, 1992.

Ra, *The Ra Material, Book I*, Whitford Press, Atglen, Pa., 1984.

Renard, Gary, *The Disappearance of the Universe*, Fearless Books, Berkeley, Ca. 2002.

_____. *Your Immortal Reality*, Hay House, Inc., Carlsbad, Ca., 2006.

_____, *Love Has Forgotten No One*, Hay House, Inc., 2013.

Roberts, Jane, *The Nature of Personal Reality*, Prentice Hall, Englewood Cliffs, New Jersey, 1974.

_____, *Seth Speaks: The Eternal Validity of the Soul*, Prentice hall, Englewood Cliffs, New Jersey, 1972.

Rodegast, Pat & Judith Stanton, Compilers, *Emmanuel's Book*, Bantam, New York, 1985.

Rogers, Ivan A. *Dropping Hell and Embracing Grace*, Outskirts Press, 2012.

Spong, John Shelby, *Rescuing the Bible from Fundamentalism*, Harper San Francisco, Harper Collins, New York, 1991.

_____, *The Sins of Scripture*, Harper San Francisco, Harper Collins, New York 2005.

Sweeney, Jon M. *Inventing Hell*, Jericho Books, 237 Park Ave., N.Y, 2014

Talbot, Michael, *The Holographic Universe*, Harper Perennial, New York, 1993.

Tarnas, Richard, *Cosmos & Psyche*, Penquin Group, 375 Hudson Street, New York, N.Y., 2006.

Tart, Charles, T., *The End of Materialism*, New Harbor Publications, Oakland, Ca., 2009.

Walker, EvanHarris, *The Physics of Consciousness*, Perseus Publishing, Cambridge, Mass., 2000.

Walsch, Neale Donald, *Conversations with God I, II and III*, Hampton Roads Publishing Co., Charlottesville, Virginis, 1995, 1997, 1998.

_____, *Tomorrow's God*, Atria Books, Simon & Schuster, New York, 2004.

Wapnick, Kenneth, *Love Does Not Condemn*, Foundation for *A Course in Miracles*, Roscoe, New York, 1989.

Weber, Renee, *Dialogues With Scientists and Sages:The Search For Unity*, Routledge and Kegan Paul, London, 1986.

Wilber, Ken, *A Brief History of Everything*, Shambhala, Boston, Massachusetts, 1996.

_____, *Eye To Eye*, Anchor Books, Doubleday, Garden City, New York, 1983.

Wilcock, David, *The Source Field Investigations*, Penguin Group, New York, N.Y., 2011.

_____, *The Synchronicity Key*, Dutton, New York, N. Y., 2013.

Williamson, Marianne, *Imagine*, Global Renaissance alliance, 2000.

Wolfe, Fred Alan and Bob Toben, *Space, Time & Beyond: Towards An Explanation of the Unexplainable*, Bantam Books, New York, 1983.

Wynn Free, *The Reincarnation of Edgar Cayce?*, Frog Books, Berkeley, Ca., 2004.

Zukov, Gary, *The Dancing Wu Li Masters: An Overview of the New Physics*, William Morrow & Company, New York, 1979.

Appendix 1

A Course in Miracles: What it is and How It Came About

Prior to 1976, if you wanted to read what Jesus of Nazareth thought or said, you would turn to the New Testament of the Holy Bible. But in June, 1976, the Foundation for Inner Peace published *A Course in Miracles*, a remarkable document detailing humanity's problems and the spiritual solution it needs. No author is listed on the title page, but a careful reading of its text, workbook, and manual for teachers indicates Jesus to be the author, but a Jesus intent on correcting the teachings, now found in the New Testament, that distort his original intent.

The book struck a chord and made publishing history. Two million copies have now been sold in English, without a word of advertising. Twenty foreign language editions have been published, with three more in preparation. It has had an impact all around the world, and yet it is safe to say the Christian Church hardly knows about it. Perhaps it is meant for those who are "spiritual but not religious," at least in its infancy.

Rather than being discovered on an ancient parchment found

buried in a clay jar in the desert, *A Course in Miracles* was received by two university professors, both brilliant research psychologists, over a seven-year period, ending in 1972, through a process of inner dictation from Jesus. It seemed the time was right for a restatement of spiritual principles to help a lost and distracted humanity, now that the discipline of psychology could help explain the resistance to love and union with God, shown in all human beings, especially in their relationships.

It is a self-study course, with a dense, descriptive text meant to stretch the mind into a broader recognition of the bind of ego vs. spirit, in which it finds itself caught. The magic is found in the workbook, as the student is asked to use 365 daily seed thoughts, over a minimum period of a year, to become more aware of the link between perception and our seeming reality, all while becoming aware of an inner voice, an inner teacher, as guide through the fearful maze we call life, toward a healing of the conflict we all feel and a better grasp of the inner peace that is our natural inheritance. The manual for teachers helps answer questions that often arise. Enlightenment is not guaranteed at the end of the workbook or in any time framework, though awakening could happen in the reading of the next sentence.

Most importantly, *A Course in Miracles* is not so much a course in learning, as in unlearning. One is not encouraged to develop one's potential, as the truth outlines our inherent perfection as God's creations. Our job is to let go of what interferes with love, so as to allow the seemingly separated parts of the Kingdom of God to reunite as one. The serious challenge that makes the reunion so tough is a combination of two beliefs: that God is to be feared and that our ego is to be trusted as our guide. We will have to learn over time to recognize the bedrock belief of the unconscious that God is our enemy is a tragic mistake, and that our ego is not our friend. We will learn to trust our inner voice for God, to heal our bitter relationships with our brothers and sisters, and come to discover an inner peace that sets the stage for God to do wonderful things for our awakening and return Home, even while still in a body.

What makes all this inner awakening possible is that we are simply returning to a state that has, in reality, never changed. What God created as whole and perfect has never truly been altered. We are simply waking up from a dream that seemed awfully real and not that pleasant. And what makes this approach so very modern and acceptable is that it works with the situation each person experiences: relationships, beliefs, perceptions, fears, guilt, judgment, criticism, and desire. What is different from a self-help fix, is that the Course student works with an inner teacher, who speaks for God. A relationship is built up over time, awakening trust, such that the power and presence of God can start to be felt and known as a friend and ally and eventually as one with the Self. The path of the ego or personality, with its techniques and approaches, is seen for what it is, the source of conflict and dis-ease. And the path outlined by the inner voice for God is revealed as one of joy and peace. The path becomes somewhat easier and more understandable.

Reading and working with *A Course in Miracles* requires a bit of split-level thinking, allowing a view that the world we see visually certainly appears real in every sense. But we allow the clarification that what we see is a projection arising from deep within our ego mind rather than a real thing in itself. It is an interpretation, based on a part of our mind that has become split off from God, and thus not to be trusted. We can learn to ask for help in perceiving our daily world differently, through the eyes of spirit, or the "vision of Christ," so as to understand how to resolve our conflicts and find healing and wholeness. Without this internal source of help and vision, we would be lost in our misperceptions. The most startling concept that unfolds, in this field of shifting perceptions, is that our brother becomes our savior. We come to discover all the hurtful events we call our grievances against our brother were only calls for help, in the deepest sense. And in responding with a loving forgiveness, we find we are healed in extending love to our brother, who is truly one with us. And in time, we discover the presence of God amidst the healing of our relationships – a veritable miracle.

A Course in Miracles is thus an inspired restatement of spiritual truths, as best perhaps that could be expressed in a conflicted dimension like our own, along with clarifications of the dark paths we have taken away from the truth, along with approaches or paths to healing to help us to awaken and experience these truths as real in our own personal lives.

We said earlier that this is a self-study course, but there are hundreds of study groups that meet weekly throughout the United States, and, indeed, throughout the world.

Bruce M. Gregory

Appendix 2

Past-Life Regression and Reincarnation

In 1972, an older friend offered to help me remember my past lives as a "pleasant experience I would enjoy." She asked me to close my eyes, take a few deep breaths, and start to focus on different parts of my body until I could actually feel a warmth or tingling sensation in each subsequent location: my feet, my calves, my thighs, etc. I found my mind calming down as she guided me through my body, and she then encouraged me to relax even more as she counted down from 10 to 1, going deeper into relaxation with each successive number. Anyone familiar with hypnosis would recognize that I was being guided into a trance, where concerns about my deeply relaxing body were disappearing, as my mind was gaining a greater focus and awareness, but at a deeper level we might call the subconscious.

She then suggested I go back to a pleasant childhood memory, a perfectly normal part of hypnotic exploration, but after that she indicated we would start exploring a life before this present one.

We eventually discovered five different periods of history that spontaneously came to mind, in which I found myself facing challenges and difficulties with people and dangerous situations that could not be considered a "pleasant experience I would enjoy." After coming out of the trance, my friend apologized for this seemingly unpleasant mental trip. I told her, on the contrary, that I discovered that each of the five "lives" (I could not prove or disprove that they were actually past lives) clearly indicated very similar behaviors to ones in my present life, after I was traumatized by bullies in the third grade, that were causing me distress, such as avoiding any potential harm from others by being guarded and defensive. I somehow knew this was a pivotal moment in my life, a chance to make a significant change for the better. I had seen the various ways I used to run away from people and danger in the past-life memories, and I had to admit I was still doing each of them in the present. Because I had already realized, prior to this past-life regression, that I was not happy with the way my life was unfolding, I was ready to reverse course, embrace life, and drop my defenses which had been keeping friends and relationships at a distance. This truly was the real beginning of the rest of my life.

Four years later, another friend suggested I get a copy of Marcia Moore's Hypersentience, as it contained a script for guiding people back into their past lives. I got the book the same day, arranged to work with a very close friend using the process the next day, and the result was a dramatic success, which helped my friend better understand his present life and relationships and resolve some pressing issues. I also found the results of one of his past lives in ancient Egypt personally intriguing, when he casually mentioned, "Oh, you were my father back then." I had grown up with the curious passion to become an Egyptian archeologist. I could not have asked for a better beginning to encourage me to help others find healing, comfort, and inspiration while exploring their past lives.

Now, not everyone understands how valuable or helpful a knowledge of reincarnation and one's past lives can be. Only 24% of the American public are believers in reincarnation, and some of the believers even question why anyone would want to know about their past lives, judging it a frivolous waste of time or simply an attempt to find past fame or glory to offset a dull, present life! Having worked with clients whose lives have been transformed for the better over the past 38 years, I can share valuable lessons from this life-enhancing process.

Perhaps the most life-changing experience that comes from working in deep trance is the reliving of one's death in a past life. You might think it would be best to avoid remembering one's death, hoping to spare the person from the ultimate trauma of suffering a violent or painful death. But the significant truth shows just the opposite. The client goes through the death experience, leaving the physical body behind, and remembers being a soul, welcomed back into the light, peace, and freedom of the Other Side. There is an immense feeling of joy and relief and a recognition that one has "come Home." It then becomes obvious that the physical life, that today is seen by materialist scientists as ending at the moment of brain death, is better described as a soul or spirit having a physical experience, to learn what past-life literature calls "the lessons of Heaven." This new identity as a soul or spirit has a transforming effect on almost every aspect of life, as one comes to believe and even know there is no death.

When a client is guided in trance to explore a past life, the narrative that unfolds is usually a personal story of events, circumstances, and relationships that lead to critical moments in that past life where powerful decisions are made about the self, about others, and even about life itself, that run counter to these "lessons of Heaven," which hold that we are all spiritual beings, created whole and perfect, and that unconditional love is our guiding life principle in all of our affairs.

The memory that comes to the client always relates to a present-life challenge, usually revealing a faulty choice of beliefs in the past life that needs correcting, but sometimes revealing a past life where the right choice was made before, so as to encourage the same nobler choice again now.

Memories of tragic deaths involving fire, drowning, or a fall from a great height often leave the client fearful of fire, deep water, or heights in the present life, until they remember the original source of their fear that reinforced their false belief that they are a body, rather than an immortal soul. They can then easily separate themselves from the seemingly irrational fears by stating, "That was then; this is now." The fears dissolve, as they no longer serve a warning purpose.

Those who have suicidal tendencies in this life may remember a very bleak past life that seemingly offered no hope to counter their desire to end their personal misery. Their past-life memory will show not only their previous suicide but also the loving reception onto the Other Side by those who will kindly counsel, "Always seek life. Never give up hope. Always call for help, and we will respond." Then suicide is no longer seen or felt as a viable option in this life.

Past-life memories may reveal the origins of carry-over physical traits that disappear once remembered. Dying of starvation in a past life may send strong signals to overeat in the present life and avoid exercise, so as to always have enough fat stored away to prevent another starvation. Coming to recognize the past life as the source of the "helpful" urges to overeat can instantly free the client from this tenaciously powerful motivation.

Traumatic deaths following severe bodily injuries often leave embedded tension in the present body where the old wound was inflicted. The rule, "To relive is to relieve," helps the client to relax that part of the body, allowing it to heal and let go of pain.

But most rewarding is the recognition, in the post-death phase of the past-life regression, that we are reunited with our loved ones, even our beloved pets, and that we reincarnate with familiar souls, who help us to continue our development of unconditional love, whether encouraging us along the way or returning into our lives to give us another chance at learning the power of compassion and forgiveness in healing broken relationships. As *A Course in Miracles* puts it, "The holiest of all the spots on earth is where an ancient hatred has become a present love."

Bruce M. Gregory
June 26, 2014, Atlanta, GA

Appendix 3

A Story of a Past Life

"Lorenzo." The vibration of those three syllables, Lor-en-zo, sent a shock wave through my body. " His name is Lorenzo." Our teacher was introducing Lorenzo, a new boy in town, to us, a roomful of third and fourth graders. I had never before heard the name, Lorenzo, but as I repeated it over and over in my mind, I experienced a pang of loneliness and almost a sense of recalling something or somebody. Lorenzo remained in our class for only a short time and I soon forgot him, but I always remembered his name.

A few years later in high school our Latin textbook had a picture of the Appian Way just outside of Rome. It showed the stones of the roadway and the caption told of the wonderful construction of the roadway, but what held my attention were the trees, the umbrella pine trees that bordered the roadway. Daily riveted to that picture for seemingly hours on end I would drift off into trance-like states and I would be transported into the scene. I was there, under those pine trees – seeing, feeling, remembering something. Those split-second flashes, as with the name, Lorenzo, left me with an inexplicable feeling of loneliness and with a strange longing.

And then, in history class, we read and talked about the Renaissance in Italy, especially of the great events in Florence. I was mesmerized again. Lorenzo! Lorenzo the Magnificent! In my fantasies I became Lorenzo, going about the City of Flowers interacting with the merchants and common folk and with the political and religious movers of the time. Then I remembered my fourth-grade short-time friend, Lorenzo.

Forgotten were my school-boy dreams and fantasies as I went off to college and then, soon after, joined the Army Air Corps. Forgotten was Lorenzo; forgotten were the umbrella pine trees; forgotten were my childish fantasies.

Forgotten – yes, until . . .

"You are coming home." I was in a military aircraft approaching Capodichino Airfield in Naples, Italy. I had never before been outside the United States. A loud clear voice was saying that I was coming home. To me, the idea was so preposterous that I tried to deny to myself that I had heard anything. When the words came, I had been looking out the window at the hillside covered with umbrella pine trees. Seeing the trees, my stomach churned with inexplicable emotion. Then I remembered the photo in my high-school Latin text of the Appian Way with the umbrella pines bordering the road. I recalled looking at that picture many times for hours on end and experiencing strange emotions, almost seeing a picture in my mind or remembering something – but what? Now I was seeing trees like those again. But why did they affect me so compellingly?

I fell in love with Napoli and with Italy and the wonderful Italian people. On an unconscious level I somehow felt that I had been there before. I felt completely at home, especially when we visited Rome, where I knew the ancient part of the city as if I had been in the habit of frequenting those streets– while in reality I was there for the first time. I didn't understand why my heart pounded with such excitement as I walked through the Roman Forum and other ancient sites. So I dismissed the excitement and feelings of awareness as just a strange experience.

• • •

It was 1964, my first day at Horace Mann School in Riverdale, New York City, where I was to teach Ancient History. I was in a lower hallway, chatting with other teachers of the History Department when a teacher I had not yet met, walked by. As he passed by, I heard a loud voice saying, "There goes Savonarola." As with the voice years earlier when I landed at the airport in Naples, the words were disconcerting. I became so visibly agitated that my fellow teachers expressed concern. But I did not try to simply dismiss those words as I had done in Italy. By that time in my life I had been reading a number of books on the subject of reincarnation and other spiritual concepts. A few days later, after I had made the acquaintance of the teacher who had passed in the hallway, I asked him whether he believed in the concept of reincarnation. His answer was, "No, of course not."

"But Bob," I persisted, even though I knew with absolute certainty how he would answer, "If you had lived before, who would you have been?"

"That's an easy question," he replied. "I would have been Savonarola of course. I always think of myself as Savonarola." Then I told him that my master's thesis at Columbia University, where I had just graduated the previous spring, was entitled "The Martyrdom of Savonarola." He became very excited, invited me to his classroom, and told me to close the door and look behind it. Hanging on the door was a large portrait of Savonarola! My head was spinning, my heart was pounding!

• • •

A few years later I was with a group on a summer expedition to Cadiz, Spain with the purpose of looking for an outpost of the fabled Atlantis. Included in the group were a dozen or so ancient history scholars, a number of young ocean divers from California, a Hollywood film crew, and a group of university students.

One day a member of the group, a celebrated psychic from

California, while meeting with me went into a trance and proceeded to tell me about a life I had lived in Florence, Italy, in the fifteenth century. She said that I had personally been involved with a preaching monk by the name of Savonarola who caused me and the city of Florence a lot of problems. At one of our meetings, she said, Savonarola asked me for permission to build a special new chapel, but because of the political situation at the time, I refused.

"Your name," she said, "was Lorenzo."

Ellwood W. Norquist

Afterword

I sincerely hope that the words of this book have relieved many from even the thought of a punishing hell. I welcome your comments. My e-mail is: philosowoody@yahoo.com

www.ingramcontent.com/pod-product-compliance
Lightning Source LLC
Chambersburg PA
CBHW050008100426
42739CB00011B/2556